I0022814

SOCIAL FUNDS:
LESSONS FOR A NEW FUTURE

Philippe Garnier
Marc van Imschoot

Copyright © International Labour Organization 2003

Publications of the International Labour Office enjoy copyright under Protocol 2 of the Universal Copyright Convention. Nevertheless, short excerpts from them may be reproduced without authorization, on condition that the source is indicated. For rights of reproduction or translation, application should be made to the Publications Bureau (Rights and Permissions), International Labour Office, CH-1211 Geneva 22, Switzerland. The International Labour Office welcomes such applications.

Title - Geneva, International Labour Office, 2003

ISBN 92-2-113511-X

First published in March 2003.

FOREWORD

In recent years, the ILO has demonstrated a growing interest in Social Funds. Their success is owed to the diversity of objectives that these unique bodies can tackle depending on the circumstances. These objectives cover a wide range including: reducing the negative impact of structural adjustment policies, fighting poverty, and creating jobs to promote women.

It was therefore natural for the ILO to become closely involved in 1992 in the creation of the Investment Fund for Development (FID) in Madagascar. Several characteristics of this Fund have been incorporated into many of those created since, including the PNAS in Rwanda and the SFD in Yemen. Between 1996 and 1997, the ILO launched a research programme on the promotion of women's employment and participation in Social Funds. The ILO also carried out a regional appraisal of the Social Funds set up in Latin America, Africa (AGETIPs), and Central Europe/CIS countries. This process was extremely valuable for the preparation of the current study, whose main objectives stand as follows:

- To perform an independent examination of the real impact of Social Funds on various ILO fields, such as job and income creation; the development of small local construction enterprises; the promotion of micro-finance operations or women's participation;

- To assess the scope in which the ILO's expertise may be better applied to strengthen the effectiveness of the Funds. This can be done for instance by involving local communities fully through training and through adjusted contract systems or by training SMEs and local consulting firms to implement projects that can create more jobs.

The aim of this study is also to encourage the application and elaboration of the model of Social Funds and AGETIPs. Social Funds have demonstrated they are effective instruments in managing the substantial subsidies of international assistance. They have done so despite their shortcomings, especially when it comes to job-creation. Today, they increasingly focus on improving their targeting of the most vulnerable groups.

The conclusion stresses that the main vocation of Social Funds is to serve as strong independent institutions that manage investments devoted to long-term economic and social development. It suggests that the ILO should become more systematically involved in designing and supervising such bodies in order to enhance their impact on employment as a top priority.

This review also recommends that Social Funds, depending on the circumstances, devise the means to:

- Reduce and prevent sustainably the risks threatening the poorest populations;

- Manage debt alleviation programmes (HIPC initiative); and,

- Incorporate special and additional programmes into the Funds' regular activities. These programmes must be set up rapidly and efficiently to cope with economic crises, the aftermath of conflicts and environmental disasters.

Special thanks go to Philippe Garnier, International Labour Office, and Marc van Imschoot, ILO Consultant, for seeing this study through. This work comes at a crucial time since many of the institutions examined by the authors are increasingly sacrificing the employment objectives for which they were originally conceived. The example of AGETIPs is a case in point. This study will also serve as a useful contribution to the debate over the future objectives and orientations of these development instruments and other means of the same type.

Jean Majeres
Chief, Employment-intensive
Investment Branch

ACKNOWLEDGEMENTS

The authors would like to thank Eddy Bynens in particular for offering his expertise on AGETIPs for this study. They also express their gratitude to Yves D'Hont, whose pertinent remarks were vital in ensuring the coherence of this document. The information provided by Angelo Baglio and Koen Delanghe on behalf of the European Union must also be gratefully acknowledged. The authors are very indebted to Piet Goovaerts and Gabriel Siri, whose knowledge of Social Funds in Central Europe, the CIS countries and Latin America, was extremely valuable. Sincere appreciation goes to Barbara Puffer-Garnier for her persistent efforts to ensure the editing of the text. Finally, this document would have remained incomplete without the contribution of Riswanul Islam, Jean Majeres and Eric de Vries, whose encouragement and advice enlightened this endeavor. To all the above, we would like to express our heartfelt thanks.

TABLE OF CONTENTS

Tables

Frames

INTRODUCTION

The birth of Social Funds is closely related to the economic crisis of the 1980's, which considerably hampered the progress of most developing economies in their fight against poverty. During this time, these economies recorded severe macroeconomic imbalances forcing them to negotiate structural adjustment programmes with international financial institutions. These structural adjustment policies were initially designed to lay the foundations for new economic growth in the short term and, after adopting programmes of economic stabilization, they were to be followed by a phase of restructuring. In practice, developing countries became mired in long periods of economic stagnation, often triggered by the decline in raw material prices and by political conflicts or environmental disasters. Moreover, the severity of political adjustment policies intensified these problems, and only exacerbated an already fragile social situation in most of these countries (Egger and al, 1992). It is within this context that, in the mid-1980s, the notion of the social costs of structural adjustment appeared. It joined the socially detrimental repercussions of restructuring measures with those that existed prior to adjustment. In 1987, this awareness was enhanced by studies conducted by UNICEF (Cornia and al) on more flexible and more humane adjustment policies and by the conclusions of an ILO High Level Meeting on employment and structural adjustment.

The challenge at that time was to conceive means and measures that could reduce the social costs of the transitory phase of economic stabilization and restructuring in a period of slow growth and scant resources. The aim was to find a trade-off that would not undermine the very basis of adjustment policies, in other words, to achieve the squaring of the circle. Moreover, the concept of structural adjustment based on deflationary demand measures in impoverished countries, usually in a cyclical low production, has been widely contested since. The World Bank of the time considered that creating Social Funds, autonomously managed, was a well-adapted solution to the two-fold requirement of protecting macroeconomic adjustment and of reducing its social costs. These policies of social compensation are all based on a set of measures involving social transfers (food subsidies, family allowances) and of direct or indirect support to employment (income-generating activities, microfinance, employment-intensive programmes and the promotion of private ventures).

Social Funds have been multiplying ever since the first[1] one was launched in Bolivia in 1986. This led to the creation of basic infrastructures, the development of income generating activities and allowed vulnerable populations to have access to social services. Their main aim was to respond to growing criticism of the impact of structural adjustment programmes on vulnerable groups. Undoubtedly, the Social Funds of the first generation constituted an attractive alternative in the short and medium term, insofar as they created a social protection net for those severely affected by economic reforms. These Funds, however, quickly proved their adaptability as they progressively developed into instruments of social policy for Governments. They were introduced in a variety of situations in countries having diverse socio-economic characteristics. They adopted one or several of the following four main themes according to the circumstances (Berar- Awad, 1997): a) reducing the negative effects of economic reform programmes in the short term; b) gaining acceptance of adjustment programmes on the political and social levels; c) finding sustainable solutions for unemployment and poverty; and d) becoming autonomous bodies able to complement the Government's social interventions at the level of local administrations and communities. This explains the variety of terminology applied to Social Funds, usually named Social Action Programme, Social Development

---

1 Several countries had already used similar initiatives without resorting to external assistance. The best known cases in point are Chili, Costa Rica, Ghana and the Maharashtra State in India. As of mid 1970s, all these countries launched emergency programs of compensation or employment that contained some of the Social Funds features. See also Stewart F. and van der Geest W.,(1994), Adjustment and Social Funds: Political Panacea or Effective Poverty Reduction? ILO, Employment Papers, No. 2, 39 P.

Fund, Investment Fund for Employment and Social Development, Emergency Fund and " Agence d' Exécution de Travaux d'Intérêt Public (AGETIP)[2] ".

Between 1986 and 2001, the World Bank approved around 100 Social Funds or similar institutions, including 15 AGETIPs in Africa. In 2001, an estimated US $ 8.5 billion, from a wide range of financial sources, had already been allocated to these Funds. The concessionary loans approved by the World Bank represented 45 percent of this amount against more than 20 percent financed by the recipient countries, especially in Latin America. The remaining 35 percent consisted mainly of loans or donations from the European Union, the Inter-American Development Bank, the Arab Fund and other fund providers such as the KFW, the AFD, the Netherlands, Japan and the USAID. As shown in Table 1, the Social Funds first launched in Latin America, spread widely throughout Africa in the 1990s, and from 1995, they gained ground in Central Europe and the CIS Countries and in the Middle East (Yemen, 1997 and Lebanon, 2001). The experiments emerging in Asia are still young and have not been taken into account in this study. Table 2 briefly describes the Social Funds in which the European Union has assumed a major role.

Social Funds have undergone steady development in the last 15 years and have become virtually permanent institutions or are considered such in practice. They are intended to tackle the structural foundations of poverty as a top priority.

This explains why the objectives of these instruments have expanded into a set of complementary activities which can tackle the causes of poverty. How is it possible to give more concrete substance to Governments' social policies, so often unable to reduce the symptoms of poverty ? In addition, where are the benefits meant to emerge from the statements and action of all sorts made by the international community, who repeatedly condemns the evil of poverty ? It is shocking after all that the number of those who must survive in the direst deprivation has been continuously growing in absolute numbers. Even though there have been

---

2 AGETIP are better known under their French acronym. These agencies of public interest works are Social Funds endowed with special features and only appear in Africa.

Table 1: An overview of Social Funds in the world from 1986 to 2000 with supporting statistics
(Financing in US $ millions)

	Central and South America and the Caribbean	Africa and the Middle East	AGETIP Africa	Central Europe And CIS countries	Asia	Total
Number of Social Funds (including AGETIPs)	13	23	(15)	11	8	70
Date of initial launching	1986	1989	1989	1993	1991	
Average life (years)	7,2	4,8	7	2,9	2,4	
Objective 1: Social protection in periods of structural adjustment	10	9	0	4	1	24
Objective 2: A durable solution for unemployment and poverty	9	21	9	11	7	57
Objective 3: Autonomous entity, relay of social policy	11	9	0	4	1	25
Other objectives: - Strengthening local capacities - Rehabilitation/construction of infrastructures	10	20	15	6	3	54
World Bank loans	1,243	1,377	412	196	548	3,776
Donations and loans from other providers of funds (including the EU)	985	1,518 (462,2)	246 (26,4)	52	128	2,929
Local resource based financing	980	553	128	32	78	1,771
Total financing received	3,208	3,448	786	280	754	8,476

Sources: Estimates made from the documents and database of the World Bank (the Social Protection Department), the AGETIPs and the European Union (amount of donations).

	Egypt: Social Fund for Development	Yemen: Social Fund for Development	Lebanon: The Fund for Economic and Social Development (FDES)	Jordan: Social Development Project
Table 2: Main characteristics of the EU-backed Social Funds in North Africa and the Middle East				
Launching year	Phase I: 1993 Phase II: from 1998 and over 5 years	EU assistance from April 2000 (agreement signed in 1998)	2001	EU assistance since 1995
Number of years of existence	Established in 1991 EU assistance since 1993	Established in 1997	Established in 2002	11 years of existence (established in Nov. 1989) operational since 1993
Objective: Social protection in times of structural adjustment	Main objective of Phase I (1993-1997)	Serves as a justification for the Fund	Reducing the social consequences of transition	Established for this particular objective
Objective: Sustainable solutions for unemployment and poverty	Main guidelines of Phase II (1998-2002)	Specifically included in the objectives	The Fund is seeking viability	Medium-term perspective and tenure to combat poverty and unemployment
Objective: Autonomous entities, a relay of social policy	Autonomous status from the beginning. They develop into permanent institutions for social development	The fund is an autonomous agency but there is no indication as to its permanent nature or its role as a focal point for social policy	The FDES is conceived as a permanent institution. It will have a special role in the policy of social development. It must also respond to the needs in South Lebanon	The objective of the Fund is to play a coordinating role in the field of small entreprise development in Jordan
Total World Bank loans in US $ millions	Phase I : 154 Phase II : 132	30	--	--
European Union donations in US $ millions	Phase I : 230 Phase II : 190	15	23	4,21
Other donations in US $ millions	Phase I : 230 Phase II : 190	15	23	4,21

Source: European Union, 2001

significant results in the past 50 years in combating poverty (Watt, 2000), these effects remain limited in light of demographic growth. In a statement made in June 2000[3], the President of the World Bank, J. D. Wolfensohn, estimated that half of the six billion inhabitants of the planet lived on less than $3 per day and 1.2 billion lived on less than $1 per day. In the entire developing world, 30 percent of adults are illiterate, another 30 percent have no access to drinkable water and 60 percent live without any sanitary installations (ILO, 2000).

Around 250,000 children under age five die every week from diseases that could be cured in these countries. Table 3 shows in absolute numbers that extreme poverty, suffered by those living on less than $1 a day, continued to rise between 1987 and 1998. The exception to this increase was East Asia, especially on account of China, in addition to the Middle East and North Africa. The spread of poverty was noticeable everywhere but was catastrophic in Sub-Saharan Africa, where in absolute numbers, it has increased 34 percent in the same period.

This means that two-thirds of Africa's inhabitants live in absolute destitution. If estimates are borne out, the world's population will increase by an additional 2 billion in the next 25 years, 97 percent of which will occur in the developing world; this is good reason for concern. Indeed, these are the very countries that already suffer most from poverty and social exclusion.

One purpose of this analysis is to examine whether, in the perspective of the ILO's social justice mandate, Social Funds can significantly ease the sustainable social integration of disadvantaged populations. Do these Funds possess the adequate range, capacity and means to produce an impact? In other words, should we foster the development of these bodies, and if so, in which direction ? The vast majority of studies conducted over the past few years - whether by the World Bank, the UNDP or the Inter-American Bank of Development - recognized the overall effectiveness of Social Funds. Yet, the model they

---

3 Second International Conference on Social Funds, World Bank, Washington, 5-8 June 2000.

Table 3: The distribution and growth of extreme poverty in developing countries and economies in transition (in millions of individuals)		
Developing countries and economies in transition	Individuals living on less than $1 per day	
	1987	1998
East Asia and the Pacific	417,5	278,3
Excluding China	114,1	65,1
Central and Eastern Europe with Central Asia	1,1	24,0
Latin America and the Caribbean	63,7	78,2
The Middle East and North Africa	9,3	5,5
South Asia	474,4	522,0
Sub Saharan Africa	217,2	290,9
Total	1183,2	1198
Excluding China	879,8	985,7

Source: World Development Indicators 2000, the World Bank, according to Chen and Ravallion

provide was also criticized[4]. Skepticism was voiced as to their capacity to create enough jobs to combat poverty. Furthermore, there was controversy on their impact on women's participation and the benefits women could enjoy.

Another purpose of this study is to elucidate why Social Funds have had different priorities, subject to the prevailing socioeconomic conditions in the region where they were introduced. For example, the most recent Funds in Central Europe and the CIS countries seem to cover the widest scale of objectives, ranging from generating employment to combating poverty by means of infrastructure construction/rehabilitation and provision of social services. In Africa, AGETIPs usually focus on creating infrastructures and generating jobs in urban areas. Until recently, the approach used in Latin America was meant to alleviate the distress of the poorest, caused by programmes of adjustment and economic stabilization.

Each of the following seven chapters was organized to point out the major trends characterizing the evolution of Social Funds in the world

---

4 For example, Tendler J., and Serrano. R. (1999), The Rise of Social Funds: What are They a Model of?; ILO (1997), Social Funds Employment and Gender Dimensions, Report on the Technical Brainstorming Workshop, ILO Geneva, 29 Sep. to 1 Oct. 1997; and, Stewart F. and van der Geest W. (1994).

and to incorporate the regional singularities involved in order to produce a useful document based on a constructive synthesis. Chapter I focuses on the original features of the Funds, their financing mechanisms, legal status and operational systems. Chapter II highlights the project selection procedures and the strict accounting methods that have undoubtedly contributed to the Funds' reputation for transparency. Chapter III weights the merits of the main activities found to various extents in the majority of Funds. These include: targeting poor populations, creating infrastructure for employment and income-generation, or assessing the impact of a Fund's activities on women. This chapter serves mainly as an inventory. Chapter IV treats in more detail the issues of decentralization, the involvement of beneficiaries and their ownership of the projects. Chapter V contains a discussion of the macroeconomic scope of Funds as well as the nature and the various phases of impact assessment studies that mark the life of a Fund. The effects induced by these institutions are also examined: for example, the possibility to use the contractual procedures used by the Funds as a model for decentralized Governments and bodies. Chapter VI examines the fields of action where it seems necessary to act in order to improve the overall effectiveness of these instruments. We will discuss in the same chapter how the Funds can stimulate greater use of the local workforce and resources. We will also examine the fields of action where the ILO has a relative advantage in terms of expertise, and how it can enhance this expertise in the operation of the Funds. In the conclusion, we start by reviewing the strengths, weaknesses and limits of Social Funds. We then suggest some areas where the ILO can constructively further the development of Social Funds and AGETIPs. The conclusion ends with a rapid overview of their future prospects in the years ahead.

CHAPTER **1**

Original autonomous institutions

I.1   Types of Social Funds and differing aims

Over the years, Social Funds and AGETIPs have grown into powerful instruments of social policy in countries in crisis or undergoing a shaky economic transition. Their main objective is to facilitate the creation of small infrastructure works, encourage the development of income-generating activities and offer better access to social services. These efforts are aimed at bolstering the fight against poverty and improving the living conditions of the poor groups, both in the rural and urban regions.

The World Bank has always played a major role in the design, set up and financing of Social Funds. These bodies act as relays, channeling the financial resources allocated by Governments and donors in keeping with pre-set procedures. To do so, Social Funds subsidize small and medium-size projects identified by local or decentralized bodies. The communities carry out these projects themselves, or delegate them to NGOs or small private sector enterprises (SMEs). They are rarely handled by the public sector. The projects financed by Social Funds are not singled out in advance, unlike more conventional projects, for which implementing agencies identify and quantify every scheme beforehand. Only the eligibility criteria are specified in what is commonly called an Operation Manual. In the same way, Social Funds are distinguished from conventional projects in that projects spring from the requests expressed at grass-roots level. Therefore, each Fund has its own special characteristics:

■ They allow for a variety in the choice of investments. In other words, they may include (or exclude) project proposals that satisfy specific criteria. These projects are submitted by public or private organizations, NGOs and community groups;

■ Projects are approved that can be carried out by the communities themselves within a system of community contract management. They may also be awarded to a delegated contract manager; in this case, Social Funds operate on behalf of the beneficiaries. The design and the implementation of infrastructure projects are delegated to local consulting firms and to enterprises. Micro-financing projects, for example, are entrusted to specialized intermediaries, such as NGOs, mutual financing institutions or cooperatives;

■ Social Funds enjoy substantial benefits, conferred by their legal status. They are endowed with an independent management and supervision, which can be exercised during the process of project endorsement. Moreover, they need not conform to the tight regulations and procedures that are in force in the public sector. Nor are they restricted by unattractive wage scales, complex procedures for awarding contracts for small local works, delayed disbursements, etc.

AGETIPs, or Agencies of Public Interest Works are a type of instrument, used only in Africa. In spite of their distinctive features (World Bank, April 1997), they are Social Funds also originally conceived by the World Bank. The majority of AGETIPs have concentrated their projects, often larger than those within Social Funds, in the major cities of countries where they operate. In addition to their role in planning investments, these Agencies are also responsible for implementing projects under a delegated contract management system. This means that AGETIPs manage projects on behalf of municipalities, for example, up until the completion of works and their final reception. AGETIPs are facing growing pressure to hand back their prerogatives to municipalities when it comes to the selection of investments. This is taking place as part of the decentralization process where there are an increasing numbers of elected Municipal Councils. AGETIPs are gradually becoming bodies which assume contract management and which entrust the design and implementation of works to local consulting firms and to the local construction industry.

Other types of projects have objectives similar to those of Social Funds. Yet, they do not enjoy a special legal status nor exemption from public sector regulations. In the amount of their investments, and in the nature of their activities they are not comparable to the projects subsidized by Social Funds. These include: the Micro-execution Programmes of the European Union, the Poverty Alleviation Programmes of the UNDP, the Programme of Support to Municipalities also of the European Union and other providers of funds as well as the Special Public Works Programmes (SPWP) performed by the ILO in the eighties.

The design of each Social Fund is closely adapted to the specific conditions prevailing in the host country. Therefore, there is a wide variety of objectives and operational procedures. A refinement of objectives has taken place in Social Funds of long standing, which have witnessed successive financing phases. This refinement takes into account previous experience and any institutional reforms that occurred in the interim. The flexibility of Social Funds is one of their principal assets.

The main development objective of the first generation of Social Funds was to reduce the negative consequences of structural adjustment policies on the most destitute groups and to contribute to local socio-economic development. It was very common for the immediate objectives to consist of:

- Creating temporary jobs by the implementation of a variety of social and economic infrastructure projects based on a labour-intensive approach (HIMO)[5];

- Generating permanent jobs while developing income-producing activities (agriculture-based activities, village granaries, cattle breeding, etc.) and micro-financing projects;

---

5 Known under the French acronym " Haute intensité de Main d'Oeuvre " (HIMO).

- Encouraging the development of enterprises in the local construction industry, particularly local consulting firms and SMEs. Training courses were organized for those concerned for this purpose. The aim was, on the one hand, to subcontract the studies to these local enterprises, and, on the other hand, to ensure the maintenance, supervision and implementation of works on the building sites. This third objective was specifically within Social Funds and AGETIPs which had already benefitted more or less directly from ILO assistance (Egypt, Madagascar, Rwanda).

In recent years, there have progressively been additional objectives in order to rise to the challenges of handing over of responsibilities to the municipalities/communities, and in order to improve on the weaknesses within the early Funds. These new objectives can be divided into three categories and aim:

- To transfer authority to communities for decision-making by helping them to become responsible for their own development and to be accountable to the population for their actions;

- To build the capacity of NGOs and local associations to foster popular participation and to help communities define, design and carry out projects;

- To train municipalities and rural communities in planning priority investments, in managing contracts awarded to the private sector, and in maintaining/operating completed infrastructures.

I.2   Institutional, legislative and organizational framework

Social Funds may be spawned from situations of crisis, whether these are economic, institutional or political. They may also be considered in countries where Governments are actively pursuing a process of decentralization (Bolivia, Honduras and Nicaragua). Thus, the institutional and legal context in which Social Funds find themselves depends greatly on the situation prevailing in the country of reference at the time of their design. Unlike comparable poverty alleviation projects within the sphere of technical ministries, under the Cabinet of the Prime Minister, or that of the President, the majority of Social Funds possess a special legal status that enables them to avoid bureaucratic red tape. This autonomy facilitates their connections with public and private agencies as well as with financial institutions, NGOs or communities and enterprises, to mention but a few. Consequently, Social Funds can draw on a wide range of strengths to fulfill their contractual duties successfully. Their status is usually that of a private, non-profit association or that of a public utility, or they may even enjoy ad hoc status, approved by a decree, which guarantees them independent management. Social Funds usually comprise a General Assembly, a Board of Directors and a General Management. The Assembly and Board of Directors are sometimes replaced by a single Steering or Orientation Committee. The task of this Committee is to adopt an overall strategy for the Social Fund, the work plans, the annual budgets and the opening of regional branches. The relations of the Fund or the AGETIP with the administration is governed by an agreement signed with the Government. This agreement sets out the rights and obligations of each party. Generally, the following bodies are responsible for the appointment of a representative to the organs of a Social Fund:

- The Government, represented by the Office of the Prime Minister or one of its key ministries;

- Technical ministries, such as the Ministry of Economy, Finance and Planning; the Ministry of Labour, Employment and Social Affairs; the Ministry of Education; and, the Ministry of Local Affairs;

- Local bodies, for example the President of the Association of the municipalities or rural villages concerned;

- NGOs involved in the Fund's fields of activities;

- Professional organizations, such as the Association of local construction industries or SMEs, the Association of local consulting firms, the Union of craftsmen, etc.;

- The beneficiaries;

- On occasion, the providers of funds, who co-finance the Social Fund;

- However, the absence of unions local construction industry should be pointed out.

This combination of diverse actors from the public and private sectors and from civil society is a unique characteristic of Social Funds. They share a common goal to fight poverty to one degree or another. They turn over the management of the Social Fund to a General Management made up of national experts, independently recruited from the labour market. The Director General is usually selected through a classified advertisement in an international newspaper while the other experts are chosen from the local labour market. A Social Fund normally operates at three levels of intervention. The relative weighting of these will depend on the total financing, the size of the country and the extent of accessibility to the zones of activity. Table 4 presents the standard organizational chart of a Social Fund.

On the national level, the General Management assumes the set-up of activities included in the Social Fund, in keeping with its mandate from the Steering Committee or from the Board of Directors. It reports on the activities and their results, and suggests work plans on a regular basis. This Management is drawn from several departments including those responsible: for community and micro-financing projects; for capacity-building of the various parties; for programming and evaluation; for computer-related monitoring; and, for the supervision of funds and internal auditing.

On the regional level, branch offices are often created, as needs arise, in order to help the community bodies to submit and to justify their project proposals for projects on the local or regional level. Another task of the branch offices is to assist these communities to constitute Project Committees and Users Associations. These will represent the Social Fund at Regional Committee meetings in order to coordinate their own activities with those of other partners, especially the decentralized government bodies. Given the wide range of projects to be handled and the many tasks attributed to the Social Funds, these branch offices are often well equipped.

On the local level, the interests of the beneficiaries are mainly protected by the (more or less) close network of community organizations, NGOs or cooperatives in place. These local bodies become responsible for the design and implementation of the projects approved by the Social Fund. They are also responsible for ensuring the subsequent operation and maintenance of the infrastructures. If a project requires specific technical skills, these local partners may delegate this task to the Social Fund, which in turn, delegates the design and implementation to local local consulting firms and SMEs.

The project receives final inspection and approval by the community and/or the municipality and the promoter at the completion of works. In countries having Municipal Councils or elected local officials, they are the ones who generally defend the interest of beneficiaries. It is not surprising then that they propose investment projects of great significance to the community. This is especially true in the case of AGETIPs.

This organizational set-up can vary over time. It also depends on the institutional reforms underway, on the amount of available investments and on the lessons drawn from preceding phases of the Social Fund concerned.

Table 4. Standard organizational chart of a Social Fund

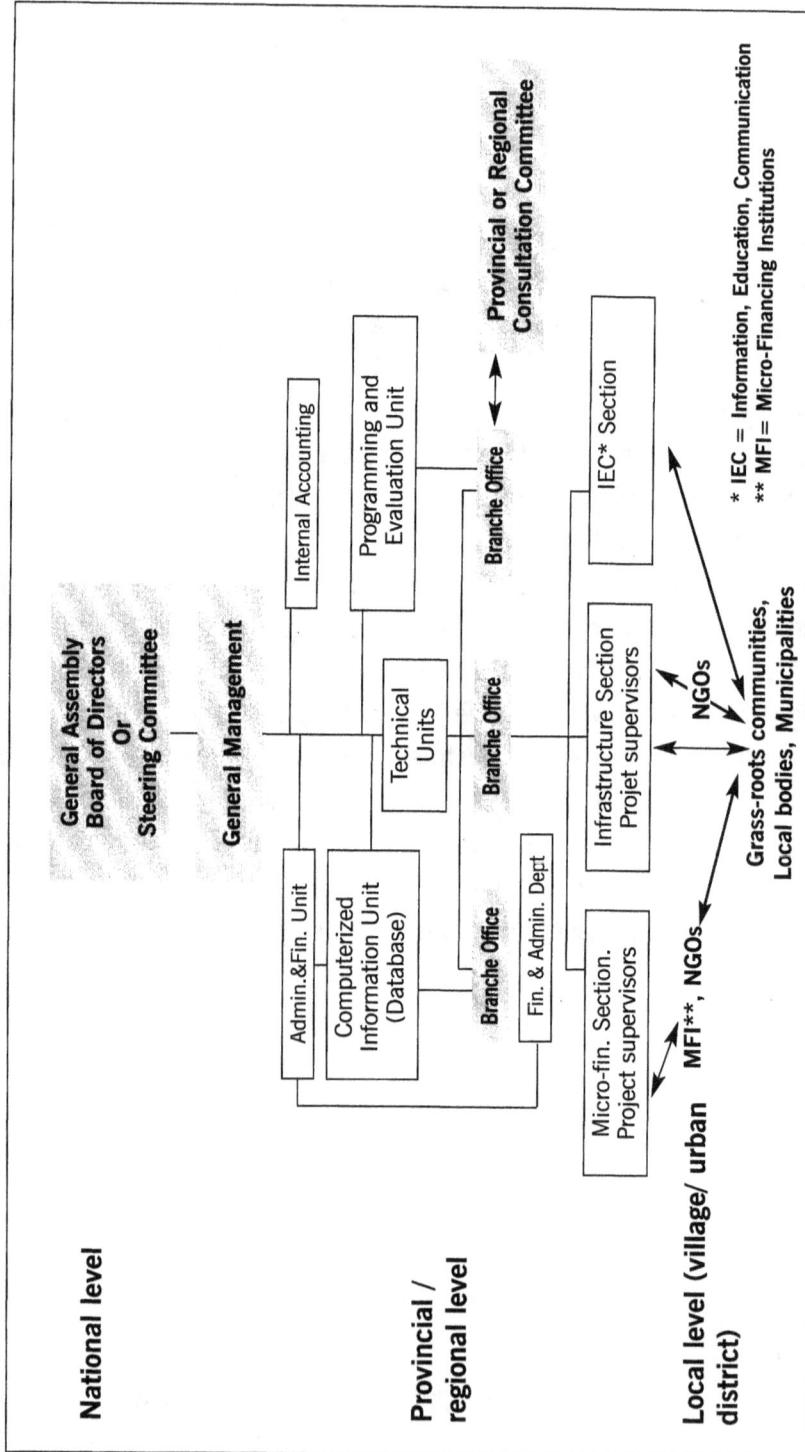

National level

**General Assembly
Board of Directors
Or
Steering Committee**

General Management

Internal Accounting

Programming and
Evaluation Unit

Admin.&Fin. Unit

Computerized
Information Unit
(Database)

Technical
Units

**Provincial or Regional
Consultation Committee**

**Provincial /
regional level**

Branche Office

Branche Office

Branche Office

Branche Office

Fin. & Admin. Dept

**Local level (village/ urban
district)**

Micro-fin. Section.
Project supervisors

Infrastructure Section
Projet supervisors

IEC* Section

Grass-roots communities,
Local bodies, Municipalities

MFI**, NGOs

NGOs

* IEC = Information, Education, Communication
** MFI= Micro-Financing Institutions

I.3 Main roles

A Social Fund assumes fairly similar functions to those of a development bank. However, the Social Fund does not grant any loans itself. Its role is only to subsidize infrastructure and training projects, and to channel funds to implementing agencies which grant credits to the different beneficiaries (for income-generating activities and micro-financing projects). Bearing this in mind, the main functions of a Social Fund can be summarized as follows:

- To chart a path for the implementation of projects that takes into account both the objectives as well as the management, cost control and measurable operational methods;

- To develop operational machinery that makes it possible to identify and evaluate the operations to be financed, to sign memorandums of understanding with the intermediaries, to conclude deals with local consulting firms and enterprises, to channel funds to operators, to monitor and pay subcontractors promptly and to evaluate project impact;

- To use a broad range of implementing agencies to the greatest extent possible;

- To promote regional consultation by putting into place branch offices. This approach facilitates a more rigorous selection of projects, identification of activities in close collaboration with the beneficiaries and a thorough monitoring of both performance and of the operation and maintenance of completed works.

Three key criteria related to the running of Social Funds deserve a more detailed explanation since they directly affect results and since they are peculiar to these specific instruments:

- First, the management costs of a Social Fund are normally restricted to 10 percent of the total budget for subsidized projects and to 5 percent for an AGETIP. However, AGETIPs still fall rather far from this objective;

- Second, the total sum of credits and grants must be divided up to cover the entire country (by province/region, prefecture or sub-prefecture) in some Social Funds. The division must be based on the population density and poverty indicators (Anker and al, 1998)[6]. The Social Fund management approves each proposal that meets the criteria, and takes into consideration the total amount of investment for each administrative zone. The project is then included in the annual work plan, based on the availability of funds. There are times, however, when this general rule is not observed, for example when it is a donor who proposes a given zone or when natural disasters occur that demand emergency action. In the case of AGETIPs, mainly operating in urban settings, this decision-making is increasingly being entrusted to Municipal Councils. These Councils usually turn to local consulting firms in order to establish priority investment plans;

■ Third, it is either the intermediaries, the communities or the private sector that assume responsibility for carrying out the various types of projects (infrastructure, credit, training). In the first generation of Social Funds, it was the system of delegated contract management that was frequently used. In this case, the Social Fund often designated local consulting firms and SMEs on behalf of the beneficiaries. Now, there are increased efforts to put the local community or municipal council in charge of contract management. The task of the General Management is solely to channel funds to these entities in several payments and to supervise their proper use. The works are conducted by the firm or the small contractor chosen by the communities. Likewise, micro-financing projects are handled by mutual credit institutions, NGOs or other intermediaries. The implementation of credit projects are assigned to SMEs. They are set up by local banks with whom the Social Fund concludes agreements. AGETIPs prefer to maintain their role as delegated contract managers for the sake of efficiency. This explains why they are the ones to draw up contracts with local consulting firms and SMEs.

---

6 In this document, the authors examine the many poverty indicators (incomes, expenses, employment, credits, etc.). They later suggest conducting basic surveys on incomes/expenses and relying on employment surveys, when available, in order to determine the zones in a country that have the highest concentration of poverty.

I.4 Funding and operation

The resources of Social Funds emanate from many sources, mainly:

- IDA credits (World Bank)[7] and other financial institutions, such as the African Development Bank, the Inter-American Development Bank, the Asian Development Bank, the Arab Fund for Economic and Social Development and the Organization of Petroleum Exporting Countries;

- Donations from providers of funds of which the most substantial come from the European Union, Japan, USAID (the United States Agency for International Development), the Netherlands, the French Development Agency, the KFW, the WFP and the European Union under the programmes of Food-for-Work;

- Various resources made available by the Government of the host country as well as equivalent funds (funds in national currency equivalent to the value of donations in kind, such as flour, fertilizers, etc.), which are sent by a donor;

- Contributions from beneficiaries themselves in various different forms;

- Recycled repayments of credits and interest due from operations regarding activities within the Funds;

- Donations received from private or public sponsors.

The proportion of international funding usually exceeds 80 percent of the total resources managed by the Social Funds. It is only in the Social Funds of Chili (FOSIS) and Guatemala (FONAPAZ) that external financing does not surpass 15 percent. Consequently, the decision to maintain, expand or reduce the activities of a Social Fund depends mainly on financial institutions and international providers.

Social Funds use the various resources listed above to finance a

---

7 The IDA (International Development Association) is one of five associations that make up the World Bank. It grants loans to the poorest countries at preferential rates. Contributions come from the richest countries and some World Bank developing member States.

wide range of small infrastructure works, micro-financing operations and training activities that meet the eligibility criteria listed in the Operation Manual. The general requirements that govern the financing of projects found in most Social Funds include the following:

- Social Funds finance only those projects that require a subsidy that falls below a fixed ceiling. This ceiling is set according to specific conditions prevailing in each country and according to the average unit costs of each type of project. For example, in the Social Fund for Developpment in Yemen, this amounts to $250,000 while in the Fund of Intervention for the Development (FID) in Madagascar this totals $50,000, except in the case of rural access roads where it reaches $100,000;

- The financing of small infrastructure projects operates exclusively by the allocation of subsidies, and it depends entirely on participation by the beneficiaries;

- The contribution of Social Funds always takes the form of an allocation of funds with the aim of injecting financial resources into underprivileged rural and urban sectors;

- Social Funds can finance the extra costs of the operation of intermediaries involved in implementation of a project up to only a certain percentage of the total cost. This means 20 percent, for example, in the Madagascar FID. However, Social Funds are not devised to fund the cost of permanent staff.

One of the important tasks of the Social Funds is to contribute to the monetarization of the rural environment by funding social and economic activities; this involves a remuneration of labour. In community development projects, however, the beneficiary population may work free of charge and offer local materials as their contribution to construction operations. In the same way, it is up to the beneficiary population to provide available sites when needed, and this comes in addition to any other contributions it may offer. The amounts, the terms and conditions of the beneficiaries' contribution are determined on a case by case basis.

The following factors are taken into account: the classification and type of project; the financing resources of the community concerned; the practices within NGOs and other development projects in the relevant area (payment in kind); the condition of the sites involved (drought-stricken area, agricultural region, etc.).

Generally-speaking, beneficiaries are asked to contribute at least 10 percent of the investment in grass-roots infrastructure costs, including equipment. This contribution has a two-fold aim. The first is to finance the largest number of projects with resources available to the Social Fund. The second is also to test the significance and priority the beneficiaries attribute to their own projects. This contribution may reach as much as 30 to 40 percent of the total cost for productive projects, such as irrigation schemes. The percentage of the contribution above concerns only the beneficiaries' share in implementation, whether it is a question of construction or rehabilitation. Once completed, the beneficiaries must assume the total cost of operation and maintenance of the infrastructure. They have different resources at their disposal to raise the sums needed. These could be direct participation of villagers, for example parents of students for a renovated school, or a joint contribution could come at the same time from the budget of the community and from a user contribution. In the case of the construction or rehabilitation of a rural access road, payment could be raised from the carriers. When there is urban development carried out in partnership with an AGETIP, it is the budget of the municipality or even the State that will make the contribution. In the Senegal AGETIP, it is the Ministry of Decentralization that provides the funds required in return. To do so, it draws upon the Equipment Fund of the local communities.

To conclude, this chapter has illustrated that Social Funds continue to reveal their unique role as bodies that marshal the dynamic powers of the public and private sectors, as well as those of civil society. Furthermore, they are endowed with broad autonomy in management, resembling that of the private sector, thus increasing their operational flexibility. The second pillar of this autonomy is composed of the strict, frequent and independent external audits. The institutional structure of Social Funds was designed so as to alleviate many shortcomings in the programmes supported by funds providers in the eighties and nineties. These included extremely slow disbursements, the limited skills of the beneficiaries for implementation and their inadequate participation in the planning stage of projects. Social Funds are generally staffed with qualified specialists, independently recruited from the labour market depending on the skills needed. This personnel is remunerated using private sector wage scales. This ensures greater efficiency in the implementation of their activities. Finally, it is important to underline the adjustment capacity of Social Funds, which takes into account important institutional reforms underway in many developing countries. Their unique institutional structure has frequently allowed them to develop into important channels of investment funds.

CHAPTER 2

Transparent management and procedures

II.1 Criteria for eligibility and project selection

The Operation Manual is the most important tool governing a Social Fund. It specifies the types of projects that can be subsidized in addition to the financing and performance criteria to be used. The goal is to provide the managers of a Social Fund with a practical reference guide that sets out its modus operandi in an accessible manner. This Manual also presents the models for memorandum agreements and standards contracts since, in these institutions, they are used in negotiations with implementing agencies and subcontractors.

Frame 1:	Main features of the Operation Manual of the Social Fund for Development in Yemen: Basic infrastructures and training activities (Volume I)

This Operation Manual comprises the following different sections:
Main characteristics of the Social Fund for development in Yemen (SFD)
Organization and function of the SFD
Sequence of sub-projects
General eligibility and selection criteria and sub-projecs financing terms
Type, eligibility and selection criteria and the results indicators for sub-projects implemented by the Infrastructures Unit
Type, eligibility and selection criteria and the results indicators for sub-projects implemented by the Water and Environment Unit
Type, eligibility and selection criteria and the results indicators for sub-projects implemented by the Social Protection Unit
Type, eligibility and selection criteria and the results indicators for sub-projects implemented by the Training Unit
Tasks of the Programming and Evaluation Unit
Procedures for the award of contracts in sub-projects
Financial management of sub-projects
Coordination between the SFD, the Government, agencies and donors

As a general rule, any major activity within a Social Fund operates under regulations stated in a specific Operation Manual. The preparation period for a Social Fund is the best time to draft an Operation Manual for each of the three main categories of activities to be found in such instruments. These include specifically: small infrastructure works; micro-financing projects and income-generating activities; and, local capacity-building programmes. The contents of each Operation Manual varies from one country to the next and are governed by local circumstances.

II.1.1   Grass-roots infrastructures

In the first part of an Operation Manual, general criteria are presented, which will determine the eligibility of a project submitted to a given Fund. In the second part, the most relevant criteria are introduced concerning the technical and socio-economic features of projects from the first category: (i) school infrastructures; (ii) sanitary infrastructures; (iii) projects of drinkable water supply and sanitation; (iv) small irrigated areas; (v) infrastructure for the sale, storage and preservation of agricultural projects, breeding and fishing; (vi) improved access infrastructures (rural access roads, road-related structures); and, (vii) environmental protection works.

The main general eligibility criteria for a project stand as follows:

- Community projects shall be retained that result from an extensive discussion among the target groups, and that reflect their aspirations. The projects are defined and proposed by the communities themselves, or in association with partners such as NGOs or cooperatives. The community is asked to commit itself firmly to the project;

- Proposals submitted must be viable from the technical and socio-economic standpoint. Moreover, projects involving social services must directly benefit the reference populations in order to justify their costs of investment and operating expenses. Productive projects must be economically and financially profitable;

- It is vital that the association, cooperative or local community commit itself to assuming the operation and maintenance of each project after its completion. Financing agreements signed with the beneficiaries must contain all the financial and institutional provisions necessary for the success of the project;
- Infrastructure projects must rely as far as possible on the recruitment of local human and material resources for their performance;
- The projects must be designed as an integral element within overall planning for investments in order to create synergy;
- The projects must benefit, as a top priority, the most underprivileged groups in a population.

The most important general criteria for the rejection of a project are:
- Recurring activities, i.e. projects devised merely to ensure the maintenance of infrastructure works that normally come under Government's decentralized technical departments;
- Highly sophisticated projects or experimental projects that would prove difficult to manage;
- Projects whose maintenance and/or operation is clearly beyond the means of the beneficiaries or the local technical departments;
- Projects that have already been eliminated from the Government's investment programme or from those of the decentralized bodies because they diverge from the development policy or because they do not fit into sector-based strategies;
- Activities that are already underway or planned within other projects or programmes. Indeed, the Social Fund must not replace available or anticipated financing sources in the project zone. It must instead complement these sources as a partner;
- Projects that are likely to damage the environment;
- A project previously subsidized by the Fund in a community and never completed. Indeed, it is unacceptable for a community to receive a second Social Fund grant if a previous commitment was not

respected for the implementation, management and maintenance of an initial infrastructure.

Requests from communities must be addressed to the regional branch offices of the Social Fund. They decide whether the above-mentioned criteria have been met. It is the department of community projects in the regional branch offices which makes a second or third selection of projects. This process depends on the technical and socio-economic feasibility of the project, and the capacity of the implementing agency. It is necessary to choose from all viable projects, to set priorities and to plan the implementation of different projects. Proposals that meet the general and specific criteria for eligibility and assessment usually far outnumber the financing and management capacities of the Social Funds. Consequently, the General Management of the Social Fund may seek the opinion of a Consultative Regional Committee, made up of the local authorities and the major development participants. This Committee will list projects submitted in order of priority based on the following criteria:

- The targeting of poor populations;
- The geographical distribution indicated by poverty maps;
- The strong commitment of applicants;
- The date of request;
- The special needs of highly vulnerable groups.

Project approval is made either by the regional branch office, the General Assembly or the Board of Directors of the Social Fund. This endorsement depends upon the cost of the project and the degree of decentralization of the Social Fund involved. Projects that are ultimately chosen are then included in the annual work plan of the Fund, in keeping with the financing available in the districts concerned. It should be recalled that the total amount of external and local financing of a Social Fund is generally distributed according to population density and poverty indicators.

I.1.2   Income-generating projects and micro-financing activities

An Operation Manual is also drafted that is adapted to this type of intervention. It includes two categories of eligibility criteria: 1) A set of criteria that apply to projects for which a financing request is made by a development body; and, 2) a second set of criteria that apply to the implementing agency (NGOs, mutual credit institutions, cooperatives, etc.). This Manual is intended to help these various bodies to define, design and manage micro-financing operations.

Frame 2:	Main features of the Operation Manual of the Social Fund for Development in Yemen: Income-generating activities and micro-financing operations(Volume II)

Fund objectives, role and intervention policy as regards credits
Criteria of identification and ex ante evaluation of subprojects
Evaluation of the capacity of the financial intermediaries
Signing of the technical assistance agreements, of the work plan and the credit and caution bonds agreements
Disbursements and administrative management
Repayment of loans
Ex-ante evaluation of different types of projects
Computerized management system

In order to be eligible, projects included in this category foster private sector development, particularly that of micro and small local enterprises. They must have firm local support and originate from a credible project developer. The latter must contribute a certain percentage to the cost of the project. This percentage, usually 20 percent of the project costs, must be paid in cash or in kind (plots of land, labour, materials, tools, etc.). A feasibility study, even a rudimentary one, is compulsory so as to ensure the viability and profitability of the operation. Obviously, projects will be refused that already meet the eligibility criteria for a regular bank loan.

Likewise, beyond the criteria for project approval, is the need to determine the eligibility of implementing agencies who will participate in organizing these productive activities. It is therefore important for them to be well-implanted in the environment and to enjoy a certain degree of credibility among project initiators and beneficiaries. They must have a competent and available staff at their disposal and an appropriate organizational and administrative structure to complement the developers' work. They must further be in a position to administer a loan or a micro-financing programme. They are expected to be able to facilitate the Social Fund's task of recovering the loans granted to the project developers. Finally, the official status of implementing agencies, in the case of an NGO, must be accepted by the authorized Government administration or by the local authorities. The frequent absence of implementing agencies noticeably complicates the tasks of Funds.

II.1.3   Local capacity-building

Social Funds often encounter weaknesses among the implementing agencies (local NGOs, SMEs, local consulting firms, mutual credit institutions, etc.). There are now means included to adapt to this situation while trying to resolve the problem. Thus, the identification of a local capacity-building project is often determined by an internal process within the Fund. This depends either on relevant indicators, on recommendations made in specific studies, such as technical auditing reports, on an impact analysis, or on an ex post evaluation. This may also result from needs expressed by the beneficiaries themselves, as in the case of cooperatives. Training courses can be organized under most Social Funds in widely varying fields, such as:

- Feasibility and socio-economic impact studies (surveys, calculation of the profitability rate, cost/benefit analysis, impact on the environment, etc.);

- Creation of an association of users, community mobilization, the creation of a maintenance fund, accounting management, etc;

- Management of infrastructures or budgeting for maintenance; training which is dispensed to local elected officials;

- Enterprise management: financial management, personnel and procurement management, organization and operation of building sites; tendering procedures;

- Technical aspects: the design of unpaved roads, labour-intensive road-building techniques, the design of small irrigated areas, etc.;
- Workshops for sharing experiences among the different regional branch offices in the same country or among different Social Funds or AGETIPs. This applies to all workshops organized by AFRICATIP, the Association that assembles the various AGETIPs in Africa.

Two main eligibility criteria are used in the selection of local capacity-building activities:

- First, the applications for training that are retained are those that include a needs justification and analysis, a clear definition of course objectives and an accurate identification of the target group. Other elements that must also be clearly specified are the course type (theoretical training, groundwork and/or school-building site), the preferred teaching method, the training equipment available or which needs to be developed;
- Second, it is necessary to check if the required training can be dispensed locally in a professional Training Centre or Training Institute by a local or international specialist, a competent local consulting firm or a highly reputable professional association with a qualified staff in the specialty. The beneficiary must also give proof of adequate knowledge of Social Fund interventions. In Madagascar for example, the Intervention Fund for Development called upon the Centre HIMO-Routes (ILO/NORAD) to train SMEs and local consulting firms in labour-intensive road-building techniques. The Entreprendre project in Madagascar offered training in enterprise management, and the Institut Supérieur de Technologie conducted the training of technicians for worksite maintenance.

II.2   Implementation and supervision of projects

A Social Fund is mainly a body which provides financing. Therefore, it does not carry out projects itself but relies on implementing agencies selected according to the category, type and size of the project. It alone assumes the general supervision of projects in order to justify its actions to the Government, its Board of Directors and the providers of funds. The design and daily operation of projects is entrusted to local consulting firms, individual consultants or implementing agencies who possess the necessary skills.

II.2.1   Grass-roots infrastructures

Two methods are used for the performance of infrastructure works, taking into account requests from beneficiaries, the size of construction sites, the technicality of the planned operations and the availability of an implementing agency. The first method consists of allowing the beneficiaries to do the works on their own using a system of community management of contracts. The second is to employ a contract management system.

Many small and medium-size infrastructure projects can be handled by the communities and are conducted entirely or partly by the beneficiaries, with the help of local small contractors. In this case, the Fund either calls upon implementing agencies who aid the beneficiaries, or it helps the community set up Project Committees made up of the beneficiaries. The implementing agency or the Project Committee undertakes to carry out the project and to use the Social Fund grant respecting the provisions of the financing agreement and appropriate administrative, financial and technical management. They are specifically responsible for ensuring in return, the organization and supervision of the worksite and of the management of contracts awarded to small contractors. They also have to purchase, store and transport materials, supplies and equipment to the site as well as to pay subcontractors and suppliers. In addition, the implementing agency or the Project Committee is responsible for bookkeeping. It must keep separate accounting for all receipts and expenses related to the project; for Social Fund contributions; the beneficiary population; and if necessary, for third parties. It agrees to facilitate the auditing of accounts by the administrative and financial department of the Social Fund. Finally, it must provide the Social Fund management with progress reports and a final report upon completion of the project. It is often assisted by a project manager or a Social Fund consultant who ensures on-the-job training at the same time. The Fund management undertakes to pay the total grant to the Project Committee or to the implementing agency according to the payment schedule in the financing agreement. The Project Committee or implementing agency undertakes to do the project and to pay the beneficiaries and suppliers directly. The role of the Social Fund throughout the project is simply to ensure the proper implementation procedures, quality control, and the general supervision of progress and of proper disbursement.

Due to the complexity of certain projects, the Fund assumes, in addition to its regular functions, the role of contract management. To this end, it enters into an agreement with local consulting firms to supervise the work and announces an invitation to tender to the local construction industry. Then, the designated beneficiary concludes an agreement with the Social Fund for the management of the contract. By this agreement, the beneficiary delegates to the Social Fund all prerogatives, rights and obligations relating to the supervision of works, studies and other essential tasks connected with carrying out the project. More specifically, the Social Fund, which is the contract manager, assumes the following tasks:

- Selects the local consulting firm and awards the contract for services;
- Supplies the relevant data and information on the project to the design office;
- Approves the technical studies: preliminary and final design studies;
- Approves the Invitation to Tender;
- Awards contracts and notifies the enterprises selected;
- Pays for services provided by the Engineer;
- Assumes provisional and final reception of works;
- Pays the final balance due for the works; and
- Pays service allowances to the Engineer.

One of the main functions of the Social Fund in infrastructure projects where it acts as the contract manager is to oversee firms who carry out the technical studies and supervise the works on his behalf. For this purpose, the Social Fund carries out surprise visits to the sites overseen by the head site supervisor. The purpose of these visits is to verify the proper performance of duties listed in the contract of the site supervisor. Social Funds and AGETIPs promote the active participation of beneficiaries in the implementation of projects, as much as possible, even if they retain overall responsibility for the operations.

This is how agreements on contract management are signed with the recipient communities. These agreements assign the responsibilities and the decision-making authority to AGETIPs in the performance phase. The communities concerned can still monitor the works and participate in weekly site meetings. They relay their observations to the site supervisor and when the need arises, to the AGETIP. However, the communities refrain from giving direct instructions to contractors. They intervene in the settlement of more specific problems such as helping to vacate building sites or to redirect traffic during the works. They also take part in the provisional and final reception of the project once the works have been completed.

II.2.2   Income-generating projects and micro-financing activities

Owing to their simple structure and reduced staffing, Social Funds cannot purport to play an important role in the definition, preparation, implementation and maintenance of income-generating projects. This is especially so, as the maintenance of these projects is more difficult and troublesome than that of small infrastructure works. This is why the Funds call upon implementing agencies to assist the developers/beneficiaries in the preparation, implementation and operation of projects (assistance/advice), and monitor their operation for the Social Funds. An implementing agency always intervenes to provide the developer and the Social Fund with "assistance/advice/maintenance" services. In most cases, the implementing agency also plays the role of a financial intermediary, either for a single income-generating project pre-approved by the Social Fund, or for small credit schemes. The Social Fund lends money to the implementing agencies for small micro-financing operations, provided they lend this money in turn to developers as small credits to pre-selected beneficiaries. The Social Fund agrees to the overall micro-financing programme and not to each project individually.

II.2.3 Local capacity-building

Within Social Funds, training activities are subcontracted to professional trainers or institutions that usually take part in training projects. The selection and recruitment of trainers is done through a selective invitation to bid. However, given the special character of these activities and the small number of experienced and qualified trainers, contracts are usually concluded by direct agreement.

Thanks to their skill or experience in certain fields, technical specialists dispense the training themselves for many Social Funds. This applies to procedures for the award of contracts and for the establishment of Project Committees, among others things. The goal is always to train local trainers who belong to training institutions and to local consulting firms, or to train individual consultants who, in turn, will be able to share what they learned with the largest possible number of beneficiaries. The quality of the training operations is evaluated by the trainees and by Social Fund specialists by means of questionnaires filled out at the end of the courses.

II.3 Managing finances and accounts

Financial and accounting management is one of the main functions of Social Funds, given that they often finance between 200 and 500 small and medium-size projects every year. Social Funds could no manage the numerous operations they subsidize without an elaborate accounting system. The main elements comprising the financial and accounting management system used are summarized below.

Social Funds must operate according to the regulations governing commercial, accounting and management systems. This obligation stems from their statutes and from the loan agreements (IDA and other providers of funds) which they sign. In this regard, the financial management of a Social Fund must fulfill four well-defined objectives:

- To assume its financial responsibilities vis-à-vis the Government, the providers of funds and the beneficiaries;

- To respect the limits of the Fund's operating costs in relation to investments;

- To apply transparent, simplified and easy-to-monitor procedures; and

- To manage and provide reliable financial information, facilitating prompt detection of problems related to project implementation, and to apply timely corrective measures.

Social Funds possess a special account in foreign currency (United States dollars) for funds from a World Bank credit (IDA). This account is credited and managed according to terms and conditions set by the IDA. Furthermore, Social Funds also have a project account in the local currency, intended for Government contributions and for the repayment of loans granted to income-generating and micro-financing projects. This special account may be decentralized to regional branch offices. The advances granted for the opening of special regional sub-accounts cover the needs of a three-month period for the regional branch offices. Re-deposit requests are made monthly or whenever the balance of the account is equal or below one-third of the advance granted. On average, a Social Fund requires new deposits from the World Bank at least once a month, and in amounts between one and two million dollars, depending on the size of the loan.

For the financings received from other providers of funds, the Social

Funds need to open other bank accounts. Thus, the European Union requests the opening of an account in Euros and an account in the local currency, both used for payments regarding all the operations.

Social Funds maintain contractual relations with numerous parties. Their prompt payment of implementing agencies and subcontractors is one of the keys to their success. It stands as a pillar of cost-control in the different types of projects. Roughly speaking, the management of the accounting is carried out in the following manner:

■ For infrastructure works and direct income-generating projects, performed with the aid of an implementing agency or a Project Committee, the Social Fund disburses the funds in several installments to a bank account specifically opened for this project by the implementing agency or by the Project Committee. The payments are made by the deadline set in the financing agreement or in the memorandum of agreement, signed between the Social Fund and the implementing agency. The administrative and financial department of the Social Fund records these payments in the project's accounting;

■ For infrastructure projects under contract management, the Social Fund pays the local consulting firms and the SMEs directly. This means that the installments are made based on the progress of work established by the enterprise, monitored and approved first by the contract manager and then by the project managers in the Social Funds. The payment procedures are listed in detail in the contracts that serve as the basic reference in accounting obligations and disbursements.

The total period between the Social Fund's reception of the detailed account and invoice, and the payment of the implementing agency or of the contractor usually does not exceed 15 days. This promptness is highly valued by subcontractors who are generally paid very late when working for public administrations. Frame 3 presents the payment schedules used in the AGETIP of Niger.

Frame 3:   **NIGETIP payment deadlines**

NIGETIP, the AGETIP implementing agency of Niger, has been in operation since the early nineties. The Operation Manual puts great emphasis on the prompt payment of invoices to contractors, setting a maximum deadline of 10 days. Two indicators are used to ensure this clause is respected:
- The average period of invoice payments to contractors; and,
- The percentage of unpaid invoices after 30 days.

These indicators are measured systematically and are included in the regular reports of the internal management supervisor. They are checked during the technical and financial audits. As an example, the values of the year 2001 were as follows:
- Average payment deadline: 7 days
- Percentage of unpaid invoices after 30 days: 0%

A few figures demonstrate the importance of keeping computerized accounting management. For example, the number of payments to be made by a Social Fund financing 500 projects per year can easily reach 3,500. It is therefore crucial to have a computerized system that automatically tracks progress of the works and payments due. This allows the local management of the Fund to monitor the operations on a daily basis.

Following procedures of the World Bank and other providers of funds, Social Funds call upon one or several account auditors every year who conduct the accounting, financial and management audits of the Social Fund. These audits check especially whether Social Funds have respected the provisions of the credit and project agreements respectively, in addition to terms of the Operation Manual procedures for the phases of implementation and standard management activities.

II.4   Transparency of procedures

Social Funds diverge from the conventional implementation systems of development projects on two very important points. First, they apply a "per programme"[8] approach. In other words, projects that need to be subsidized are not pre-selected. Second, operation and management procedures are designed to guarantee the transparency of the Funds in all their interventions.

With regard to project implementation, the beneficiaries are involved

---

8 This highly beneficial improvement in the financing methods for development aid is increasingly found among international donors (i.e., DANIDA), because it facilitates greater flexibility of action.

to the maximum in the definition, selection and performance process. Requests are reviewed in consultation with the beneficiaries at the village level to ensure that these reflect the wishes of the majority of the population. The performance of simple projects is handled by Project Committees whose members are chosen by the population. In the same way, the management of small contracts is entrusted to these Committees. To this end, these Committees can seek on-the-job training on how to organize an association, keep simplified accounting and administer small contracts. When the system of contract management is used, the beneficiaries, acting as works' supervisor, are represented during the opening of bids in the Technical Commission. This Commission includes the Director of the Social Fund or his representative, the Project Manager, the local consulting firm and the works' supervisor, among others. The task of the Technical Commission is to evaluate and compare between offers. The general philosophy underlying Social Funds is to convince the populations where they operate that the funds granted are being used in a collaborative and transparent manner.

The credibility of Social Funds in the award of contracts for works and procurement is grounded in the presentation of clear, detailed specifications provided in the technical and financial tender documents. This credibility depends greatly on the training of SMEs in this field, and on the opening of bids in the presence of the contractors and the beneficiaries' representatives. The award of contracts in the community management approach comes under the Village Supervision Committee. This body operates independently from the Project Committee, which Is responsible for the implementation of the project.

Project supervision is handled at several levels and assumes several forms. This task is undertaken by:

- The Village Supervision Committee, whose members are elected by the population;
- The local consulting firms or the individual consultants recruited by the Social Fund to handle a specific project or a set of projects;
- The Project Manager from the Social Fund who works in the regional

branch office of the Social Fund, and who is in charge of the technical and financial aspects of the projects;

■ The department in charge of the three main categories of projects on the level of the General Management of the Fund, and whose mission is to supervise the activities of the regional branch offices.

The general supervision of the activities of a Social Fund falls to the Board of Directors who approve the work plans and budgets, the progress reports (quarterly or half yearly) and the audit reports. The technical and financial audit reports are required by the providers of funds. The annual technical audit monitors whether the Social Fund has respected required procedures, quality of the works or services, unit costs of the projects and rules for the award of contracts. Furthermore, beneficiaries are occasionally interviewed to check if the projects approved truly fulfill their expectations and if they were involved in each phase of the project.

Finally, despite the particularities of each Social Fund, the Operation Manuals increasingly incorporate a common set of elements: these extend from selection criteria for projects to standard contract models and the methods of awarding project contracts. This enables the Funds to get a head start and guarantees greater transparency in technical, accounting or financial operations. This transparency also characterizes the methods used to engage communities in the different stages of project implementation.

Moreover, operations in most Funds are highly computerized and have one or more databases available in modular form. Among other things, a module is created for each of the project's important data. This concerns mainly financial data, information on the various participants (local associations, SMEs, local consulting firms, suppliers, etc.) and poverty indicators. All this information enables Social Funds to administer and commit a substantial amount of funds well beyond the possibilities of other development methods. Indeed, one of the obstacles faced by international aid arises from the difficulty of spending the funds allocated to a development project within a reasonable time frame. It seems that the Social Funds do a better job circumventing this difficulty (Jorgensen,Van Domelen, 1999).

CHAPITRE 3

Various activities with divergent results

III.1 Target groups: poverty alleviation activities

At the outset, the subsidies and services administered by Social Funds are directed to a targeted group of beneficiaries, selected amid a larger population. Targeting key groups remains, however, an operation with political overtones, although this may be regrettable. This process is very little appreciated by the Governments. It is a thorny issue to choose certain families or individuals over others. This is especially true when those excluded belong to a prominent group that may be influential in the area of activity. Well aware that most poor people are scarcely represented, Governments are more reluctant to make them the most direct beneficiaries of their action (Marc and al, 1993). Bearing in mind possible imbalances owing to this fact, target groups usually include (Berar-Awad, 1997): (a) the "new poor", i.e. groups affected the most by an economic stabilization and reform programme linked to cyclical necessities; (b) groups living in chronic poverty and constantly trapped in its vicious circle; (c) the most disadvantaged groups, such as women heads of household or illiterate girls; (d) workers affected by a reform programme in the public sector or by a process of privatization; and, (e) the various categories of unemployed.

The process of identifying target groups used by Social Funds can be carried out in the following ways: drawing up of poverty maps; by using criteria of the "self-targeting" approach in which target groups identify themselves; or by conferring this task to intermediaries, such as the implementing agencies. Each approach has its own rationale and relies for this task on several indicators. These indicators must be easy to use and eschew costly surveys:

■ The mapping approach is used to concentrate the activities of a Fund in a given administrative district or region of the country. To achieve this, a combination of indicators is used including: poverty indicators, access to certain basic social services, the dietary and sanitary levels, the infant mortality rate, the literacy rate, etc. This approach is frequently used in Social Funds in Latin America but much less in sub-Saharan Africa where reliable data are scarce, thus preventing this process from being truly effective;

■ The "self-targeting" approach in which target groups are supposed to identify themselves consists, for example, of setting a maximum salary for labour-intensive infrastructure works done by public works departments. This applies to the basic infrastructure works performed by the Promotion Nationale[9] in Morocco. Alternatively, the law of supply and demand determines the level of the salary when the works are carried out by a firm. Therefore, it is difficult to supervise a contractor who won a bid from a Social Fund and who is supposed to hire a specific type of manpower. This contractor may insist that paying a higher salary would allow him to recruit better skilled workers, hence more productive. This approach can also determine the maximum amount of loans granted within a micro-financing programme, or the specific components of food aid programmes;

■ Recruiting implementing agencies allows the Social Fund to rely on a body that knows the target groups very well, and is therefore able to make a better selection. However, it is often difficult to find NGOs with true grass-roots connections, or to find cooperatives and other experienced development operators, especially in remote regions.

---

9 The Moroccan Government allocates around $50 million every year to a large scale labour-intensive programme. Seventy percent of the funds are used to pay workers using the scale of SMAG (Minimum Agriculture Salary), which amounts to $4 for each working day.

Almost half of the existing Social Funds (Owen, Van Domelen, 1998) stipulate that one of their main objectives is to benefit poor populations. Nevertheless, they usually describe these target groups in rather general terms. Very few of the early Funds had measurable indicators to identify such groups accurately, since most of them had set only short-term objectives. In spite of these shortcomings in earlier Social Funds, and regardless of their lack of coherent methods, an evaluation made by the beneficiaries between 1989 and 1996 (Owen, Van Domelen, 1998) confirmed their impact on the poor. The preliminary results of a recent study conducted by the World Bank (Rawlings and al, 2000) in six countries that have active Social funds (Armenia, Bolivia, Honduras, Nicaragua, Peru and Zambia), demonstrate more convincingly the actual capacity of Funds in identifying the most vulnerable groups. The study concludes that the Funds under study benefit the poor populations and affirms that the targeting process improved over time.

Frame 4:   **Targeting poor populations in some Social Funds**

Some 76% of Social Fund resources in Nicaragua were collected between 1991 and 1998 to assist municipalities living with high or extreme levels of poverty, (i.e., 53% of the population);
More than 80% of subsidies were granted to 40% of the poorest municipalities in Peru between 1992 and 1998;
In Honduras, 51% of funds benefitted two categories in the poorest municipalities (described as poor and very poor and including 41% of the population) between 1994 and 1997 (2nd Social fund).

Undoubtedly, the main concern within the majority of Social Funds is to benefit the poor, if not the poorest. Obstacles still persist, however, which prevent the systematic use of better targeting techniques, such as:

- The weight of the political factors which, in practice, often force the Social Fund to intervene on the entire territory since every region is affected by poverty, though to varying degrees;

- The size of Funds which remains too limited compared with the need, and thus hinders the targeting process; and

- The considerable effort required to remedy the qualitative deficiencies of the projects submitted by the poorest and most isolated beneficiary groups.

Even though there is now more accurate detection of these groups and, Social Fund authorities are obviously favorably disposed towards them, by definition, the beneficiaries rarely have the technical ability to come up with articulate project ideas. This is why the majority of Social Funds include campaigns of information, education and communication to help beneficiary groups submit their requests and design projects.

These contradictions were brought to light as regards Latin America (Siri, 2000). This is a complex issue and the area where size can intervene because the larger a Social Fund, the better its chances of reacting the key target-groups in a more egalitarian and lasting manner.

Despite the differences between countries, the majority of Social Fund grants (Ebbe, Narayan, 1997) are divided in the following manner: a) around 90 percent for small basic infrastructures, two thirds of which go to social infrastructures and one third to productive, economic and protection infrastructures; b) 5 to 8 percent for micro-financing operations; and, c) 2 to 3 percent for capacity-building programmes. These numbers were collated from the 51 Social Funds in which the World Bank was involved in 1996. This evaluation (Rawlings and al., 2000) confirms that target populations have significantly greater access to schools, care centers and to water and sanitation works following the construction and the rehabilitation of the corresponding infrastructures. This means that the social objective of the funds is usually reached.

In a recent study by the ILO (van Imschoot, 2000), it was estimated that Social Funds and AGETIPs in Africa have a greater impact on unskilled unemployed workers and on those who are under-employed throughout the year or intermittently. Undeniably, Social Funds offer these target groups more opportunities for employment and on-the-job training because of the nature and the volume of subsidized operations.

At this stage of the study, we can attempt to offer a few observations on the quality of the targeting within Social Funds and on their impact on the priority beneficiary populations:

- There is regular improvement in the targeting and assessment of key groups;

- The projects within the Social Funds's spectrum of interventions are such that it is not only the poor and vulnerable who benefit but also those who are noticeably better off;
- Compared with the overall set of activities within Social Funds, there are too few projects, and specially too small, that are liable to create lasting benefits for the poorest populations.

Despite all their advantages, Social Funds have yet to encounter the approach that would enable them to have a more systematic impact on the poorest people. Indeed, these programmes are not simply subsidies; they are programmes meant to produce lasting benefits for development. It is even more difficult for such programmes to benefit the most marginalized populations. Without rejecting current methods, additional efforts nevertheless need to be deployed, first. These must improve the targeting process and its assessment, and secondly, a better balance is needed between productive projects vital to long-term development and specific projects enabling vulnerable groups to break the vicious circle of poverty, without becoming welfare dependent. This task has been so far relegated to other aid programmes. We will refrain from being too critical of Social Funds in this area because they compare favorably with other poverty alleviation programmes financed by the UNDP, which have higher costs of operation. The same problem arises in Social Funds recently set up in Central and Eastern Europe and in countries of the ex-Soviet Union. Even if there is a lack of substantiating data in this matter, it has been estimated that in these regions also, Social Funds have tangible consequences on the poor, although very modest ones on the most destitute (Goovaerts, 2000).

III.2 Employment and income creation

Income and job creation are one of the relatively explicit objectives of Social Funds and AGETIPs. Latin American Funds were established in the first years with the priority of creating temporary jobs to counteract the detrimental effects of stabilization programmes. However, soon afterwards, the majority of Funds were designed to create more lasting jobs:

■ The Operation Manuals stipulate that the selection of basic infrastructures must meet a specific set of eligibility and rejection criteria. For this purpose, they recommend using scoring charts. Preference is given to construction and rehabilitation operations that can make best use of local labour, materials and know-how. The use of sophisticated materials, usually imported, or the choice of projects not technically designed to use labour-intensive methods will be excluded, or at best, poorly graded. Similarly, the recruitment of local small and medium-size contractors, who are readier to apply the methods required, will be preferred. Certain types of projects such as irrigation schemes or local markets generate their own employment in the long term in contrast to projects of social value that can operate only with a budget from the Government, or from the decentralized communities, and that require users contributions;

■ Micro-financing projects generate lasting jobs and incomes. As they remain small and few within Social funds, this prevents them from exerting a noticeable impact on employment;

■ Capacity-building activities involve NGOs and local communities as well as engineers, technicians and managers from local consulting firms and SMEs that are subcontracted. Developing the technical and the management skills of all these participants has almost immediate effects on employment, since even at the project design stage, one observes an increase in the use of local resources, both in men and materials. This "employment" effect is reinforced in the longer term by the improved capacity of all the technical and management staff.

Frame 5: **An overview of the main components of employment-creation in small infrastructure projects**

- Short-term employment pertains to the construction/rehabilitation phase of a project. The following can usually be distinguished:
- Direct primary employment does depend on the nature and total amount of the investment, but above all, the choice of the construction technology selected. To give a rough estimate of relative cost, and assuming equivalent technical specifications and quality, calculations showed that the rehabilitation of one kilometer of rural access roads in Lesotho and Zimbabwe (Lennartson, Stiedl, 1995) cost respectively 37% and are 7% less with an employment-intensive method (HIMO) than with an equipment-intensive method (HIEQ). In terms of economic cost, the HIMO approach represents half of the HIEQ cost in Lesotho and 79% in Zimbabwe. The percentage of the labour used in both countries totals nearly 40% of the entire cost for the HIMO approach compared to 6% (Lesotho) and 13% (Zimbabwe), respectively with the HIEQ approach. Furthermore, the number of days/work required to rehabilitate a one-kilometer length of rural access road, using the HIMO method, varies from 1,500 to 5,000, depending on the terrain and the extent of work, 80% of which being unskilled labor. With the HIEQ method, implementation takes three to four times less. This difference is not usually significant for this type of works in the rural environment. However, if this factor matters, the works can be subcontracted in several segments to three or four firms;
- Indirect primary employment precedes implementation and comprises the production and the transportation of elements indispensable for the construction operations. When local resources are used to the maximum (stone, tile, brick, paving stone, manufactured locally tools, etc.), which is especially true in the construction of buildings, paving and sanitation works in the urban environment, this indirect primary employment can amount to 10 to 20% (Guérin, 1994) of the direct primary employment in this type of works;
- Induced employment results from new employment opportunities or from the expansion of existing jobs due to the workers' consumption of the different projects in the zone concerned;
- Durable employment arises from the operations phase of the project. In terms of the number of jobs created, it is customary to classify the works that are directly productive at the top. Usually, economic or access infrastructure projects follow rural access roads and bridges, for instance, with social investments bringing up the end. This classification follows the same pattern as profitability criteria for the projects. Undoubtedly, social investments create few permanent jobs apart from those related to the operation and maintenance, which mean high overhead costs for the community or region concerned. These investments, however, are crucial since providing basic social services is a key to fighting poverty. This highlights why Social Funds need to strike a balance between the different types of projects and their geographical distribution so as to maximize impact.

In practical terms, the Funds' contribution to employment creation has been relatively modest in Latin America (Siri, 2000)[10]. This stems partly from a deliberate policy of subcontracting project works in a concern for efficiency and to ease the administration of Funds. This is a praiseworthy policy in itself and should even be recommended provided it includes contractual obligations for the contractors. For instance, to foster employment creation, particularly by local recruitment of unskilled labour. However, this has seldom been the case in Latin America. Wages as a percentage of the Funds' total expenses did not usually exceed 25 percent. This is low indeed, even in Latin America, where labour-intensive infrastructure works are fairly well known by the rural communities, even if they are less commonly used than in Asia. The costs of labour in these works must normally be set between 25 to 50 percent of the overall budget, depending on the type of construction or the infrastructure. The creation of steady employment has been equally low according to the few estimates available[11]. This is the result mainly of the development of micro-enterprises that received loans. Yet, micro-financing activities make up only 5 to 8 percent of total activities within Social Funds. Ultimately, the creation of durable employment seems to derive most from wages and expenditures generated by the Funds. A study conducted in 1989[12] revealed that 22,000 jobs resulted from the economic expansion generated by the Bolivian Social Emergency Fund.

Rarely have we come across any detailed review of the impact on job creation of the various activities within Social Funds in Africa. The data provided in Frame 6 concerns Madagascar and Rwanda, where significant job-creation, especially of temporary jobs, took place. The same can be noted for the Egyptian Social Fund where a 1997 study revealed that 50,000 to 70,000 jobs were created every year (Kheir-El-Din, 1997).

---

10 In this study, the author proceeded to calculate the creation of jobs in 11 South American Funds between 1990 and 1995. Apart from the Honduras Fund (0.8 percent), he concluded that the annual percentage of employment generated by the Funds in these countries was an average of 0.2 to 0.3 percent.

11 For example, the proportion of workers from the construction sector in Peru who found a job after working in the FONCODES (Fondo Nacional de Compensacion y Desarollo Social) did not exceed 2.8 percent, according to a consultant's report at the Inter-American Development Bank (Moncado Vigo G., 1997, p 212).

12 These are the results of a general equilibrium model of the Bolivian economy, prepared in 1989, on the impact of the Social Emergency Fund.

Frame 6: **Employment-creation indicators in the FID II in Madagascar and the PNAS in Rwanda**

Madagascar (from July 1996 to July 1998): 1,773,791 days/work, which is approximately 8,000 years/work of temporary jobs compared with 345 permanent jobs created each year from micro-financing income-generating activities. It is worth mentioning that the cost of creating one permanent job is 3.5 times higher;

Rwanda (from 1995 to 1998): 630,000 days/work, which is approximately 2,625 years/work of temporary jobs compared with 200 permanent jobs every year, derived from income-generating activities. In Rwanda, the cost of creating one permanent job is five time greater.

Job creation has remained an important objective in AGETIPs, although this goal has evolved over time. The predominant aim of the early years, which set short-term employment as a determining factor for these agencies, has broadened into a larger plan. Municipalities are increasingly aware of the marketable profitability of projects and of their impact on sustainable development. Consequently, the choice of projects is not founded solely on the various kinds of employment creation that can be expected. Nevertheless, the example offered by the NIGETIPs tends to prove that this remains an important objective for them.

Frame 7: **Employment creation in the NIGETIP agency**

NIGETIP constitutes the urban portion of the World Bank-led Infrastructure Rehabilitation Project (PRI) in Niger, and it funds the implementation of works conferred on this agency. One of its important objectives is to create jobs, using as indicators both the percentage of infrastructure costs spent for wages and the number of days of work created. Works supervisors are responsible for recording these data. In 2000 and 2001, the percentage of labour costs relative to total expenses amounted to nearly 26%. This is a relatively high figure, given the type of works carried out by this agency.

NIGETIP also uses many local materials produced outside the building sites, and these, in turn, require a local workforce (carpentry, metalwork, gravel, sand, etc.). This agency also records the percentage of local materials used in the projects it subsidies. This percentage totalled 33 percent for the years 2000 and 2001. If we estimate the percentage of labour costs in the total cost of local materials used at 25 percent, this will increase the share of labour in the total cost to nearly 34 percent. This figure does not include the induced employment in the other sectors concerned of the national economy.

In contrast, the statistics are less reliable for the number of workdays. Moreover, there is no available information on the distribution of wages between men and women, or between the different categories of workers. These data would certainly be very useful in evaluating the impact of the AGETIP-implemented projects on poverty.

Despite the " youth " of Social Funds in Central and Eastern Europe and the ex- Soviet Union, there seems to have been only marginal job-creation to date. This fact can be attributed to the Soviet legacy, characterized by excessive mechanization and a glut of equipment for public works. A certain reluctance persists with respect to labour-intensive work. In these highly mechanized economies, the cost of using this wealth of machines remains attractive while the profitability of the labour-intensive construction methods is not always obvious. While Social Funds are highly appreciated in these countries, one must realize that they rarely use unskilled labour. This is inconsistent with their stated aim of assisting the poorest groups. The Social Fund created in Armenia in 1998 provides a good illustration of this paradox (Goovaerts, 2000).

Social Funds are set up to have a computerized management and monitoring system for the various activities, which creates a link between expenses and concrete results. This system provides a clear picture of the direct jobs created, among other things. Nevertheless, special studies would be required to obtain a proper estimate of the number of permanent jobs created and generated by the Funds work. To our knowledge, no study of this type has been done. The results of the study conducted several years ago in Madagascar (Razafindrakoto, 1999) are however of interest. This country developed a simple macro-economic model of the Malagasy economy to simulate the impact of all labour-intensive and capital-intensive investments. Although this research covered more than just the FID and AGETIPA, it showed that, for the period 1990 to 1995, labour-intensive projects created two to three times more jobs than projects that used more conventional methods. Similarly, little attention has been given local SMEs and local consulting firms that benefit from contracts for construction work and for feasibility studies within the FID and the AGETIPA. Such an evaluation could have determined the employment benefits induced from these contracts and from the training received in this connection.

Undeniably, employment creation was a major objective of the earlier Social Funds in Latin America, especially to help reclassify workers who lost their jobs in economic reform programmes (Wurgraft, 1995). This objective remains a priority in the Social Funds of Bolivia[13] and Mexico. This is also the case in the Egyptian and Malagasy Funds where the ILO has been noticeably involved since 1993. It remains a key objective in AGETIPs as well, although somewhat less than previously. Job creation objectives seem less important in the Social Funds of the second generation although the examples cited in this document inspire a more moderate judgment. However, when there is a lack of reliable data, the impact on employment is sometimes difficult to demonstrate. What further complicates the situation is the fact that the Social Fund personnel lack time to verify the accuracy of data pertaining to job creation provided by the local consulting firms or other partners.

III.3 Impact on women

Social indicators show that women are more exposed than men to the hardships of poverty and that, as the years go by, these disparities are further accentuated. Women account for 70 percent of the 1.3 billion people living below the line of absolute poverty in the world. More than 80 percent of men of working age are economically active, compared with only 55 percent of women[14]. The female population harbours a wealth of skills and talents waiting to be tapped. Women were particularly affected by the successive economic recessions in Latin America of the eighties, as well as by the ensuing cuts in social budgets. In this part of the world, the percentage of women who are head of household reaches 20 percent. Indeed, over the past few years, women have been increasingly encouraged to seek an activity outside the home, which has considerably increased their participation rate. Unfortunately, they often hold jobs in the informal sector, both low in pay and in productivity (ECLAC, 1998). The situation of women is even less enviable in Africa where their rate of employment in the formal sector is the lowest in the world, while they are the majority in the informal sector.

---

13 In Bolivia, the Emergency Social Fund gradually gave way to a Social Investment Fund in which the diverse employment objectives are readily identifiable..
14 According to the Human Development Report, UNDP, 2000.

Moreover, they work mainly in agriculture in poorly paid and seasonal activities. As in other regions of the world, women have suffered greatly from economic reform programmes. They remain particularly uninformed of their fundamental rights. They are often the most severely affected by the consequences of the conflicts that have long caused bloodshed in Africa. Finally, the feminization of poverty may well be the most worrisome aspect of women's condition in this continent.

It is not surprising that Social Funds designate women as one of the priority aims in their interventions, given their extremely dire situation. It remains to be seen, however, whether this practice lives up to expectations, whether women participate in decision-making, whether they are recruited in projects within the Funds and whether they eventually benefit from them. The following analysis is based largely on the conclusions from the Programme implemented by the ILO in 1996-97[15] to evaluate the effects of Social Funds on women.

As previously mentioned, nearly 90 percent of the grants from the Funds focused on basic infrastructures, almost two thirds concerned social services while only 5 to 8 percent went to micro-financing projects. This distribution has negative consequences on women. It is generally men who are hired for construction jobs even if this is temporary work. This is usually considered normal in the construction industry, given the difficulty of the tasks. Women do not share this view, but their opinion is rarely sought in the selection of the most urgent projects because they are traditionally under-represented in the local decision-making bodies. Moreover, they are not automatically guaranteed equal access to the benefits of social infrastructures such as schools and care centers. In this connection, families with low income give priority to the education of boys for cultural and economic reasons, even if education fees are the same for boys and girls[16]. A wider range in the

---

15 ILO, Social Funds: Employment and Gender Dimensions: Report on the Technical Brainstorming Workshop, Geneva, 1998. During this meeting, conclusions were drawn from the results of seven case studies, conducted in Bolivia, Egypt, Honduras, Madagascar, Mexico, Peru and Zambia.

16 These statements emerged from a discussion between the representatives of several Social Funds, who gathered at a seminar from 29 September to 1 October in 1997 at the ILO in Geneva. This seminar centered on the implications of Social Funds for women (Social Funds Employment and Gender Dimensions: Technical Brainstorming Workshop).

selection of projects, which women would have a say, would allow them to gain more from the projects. For example, encouragement is given to build separate schools for girls in certain Social Funds, such as in Yemen, so as to incite parents to educate their daughters. On the other hand, it must be acknowledged that certain projects commonly found in the majority of Social Funds benefit women more than men. This is true for water and sanitation projects that have many advantages: women have to walk shorter distances to fetch water, which saves time and improves sanitation. The same is true for the construction of covered markets, which provide better and cleaner conditions for women to sell their wares.

Frame 8 contains a description of the experiences in Madagascar and Rwanda, where concrete measures have been taken to engage the participation of the neediest women in various infrastructure, rehabilitation and sanitation works.

Frame 8:	**Urban development works for the most underprivileged women**

The ILO and the WFP, in collaboration with the Government of Madagascar and the World Bank, designed the "HIMO Urban Works", a custom-made programme to assist poor women living in the capital, who often are heads of households. The "HIMO Urban Works" was a component of the SECALINE[17] project (Food and Nutrition Security) to which the Intervention Fund for Development was initially affiliated. The works consisted mainly of cleaning out drainage systems in the poor sections, cleaning open lots and ponds and carrying out other small works in the city. The target group was successfully assembled mainly by means of offering payment in kind rather than in cash, men being more appreciative than women of cash payment. The value of the food ration was equivalent to the minimum wage and a limit was set of 5 working hours per day so that women would be also able to attend to their domestic tasks or do other small jobs. Around 1.3 million workdays were generated in this way from 1993 to 1997, 70 percent of which benefitted the most underprivileged women.

The second example concerns the National Programme of Social Action (PNAS) in Rwanda. This fund was restructured in the aftermath of the 1994 events. Numerous jobs in the building construction sector were assigned to women owing to the scarcity of men. Between 20 to 30 percent of the jobs created under this Fund were given to women, at the same wage scale as that used for male workers.

---

17 SECALINE: The Madagascar Food and Nutrition Project. Refer to the final implementation report, the Republic of Madagascar, World Bank, credit 2474/MAG, 1999.

Social Funds are distinguished by a selection of projects negotiated with the beneficiaries. Such an approach implies that the needs of women, among other target groups, will be better taken into account. In fact, women who rarely have the right to speak out and who are not used to expressing themselves within the local communities, find themselves deprived of a voice and of any involvement. It is the husband, father or the prominent villager who usually represents them. Thus, in the majority of Social Funds, it was possible to pinpoint the main factors that complicate women's attempts to express their preferences. This is caused by: prevailing socio-cultural considerations in each context; the low literacy rate; the difficulty communicating and expressing oneself in public; a very low social status; the right reserved by men to speak on behalf of the whole community; women's lack of confidence in their ability to speak their mind and to manage a project; and by the barrier that intermediaries or Project Committees raise between women and the Social Funds' representatives.

To deal with this reality, Social Funds now include certain actions for improving women's participation in these activities. Thus, the quota system was introduced in Zambia to allow better representation of women in the local Committees that negotiate projects for the Social Fund. Savings and loan projects and income-generating activities were specifically designed for women in Yemen[18]. In late 1999, women made up 48 percent of micro-financing project beneficiaries in this Social Fund.

These examples reveal that Social Funds have demonstrated awareness of the enormity of this challenge set in an unfavorable context for women's promotion. Efforts are being stepped up to promote women's participation in the cycle of projects. In spite of these attempts, resistance persists in the local environment, and the results obtained in this respect are not solid. It is necessary to recognize that women are still victims of severe discrimination. It is difficult for them to impose their preferences, much less their rights. They do not enjoy enough of the project benefits. Increasing the number of micro-financing projects can significantly strengthen women's role and multiply the advantages they

18 Annual report 1999, Social Fund for Development, Republic of Yemen.

may reap from Social Funds, as the next section of this study will demonstrate.

III.4 Micro-financing operations

The purpose of micro-financing[19] institutions is to offer financial, savings and loan services to very poor people. Their aim is to generate sustainable jobs and incomes, and to facilitate the economic and social integration of the beneficiaries. It comes as no surprise then that a certain number of Social Funds came to integrate this type of operations into their financing system. Chapter II demonstrated how the Funds can work with intermediaries who are able to manage a micro-financing operation, in order to help implementing small income-generating projects that directly benefit developers, the communities or individuals. This is precisely the objective of micro-financing operations: to develop the skills of independent workers, finance income-generating community projects or to foster the creation /development of small enterprises.

It was in the eighties that micro-financing operations started to assume their new familiar characteristics. It became obvious that people who lacked access to conventional instruments still needed a wide range of financial services. This situation similarly required a greater variety of means for repayment. An effort was also made to designate populations who would otherwise be forced to seek alternative financing in the informal sector with all the associated risks, such as prohibitive interest rates.

Based on an evaluation made by the World Bank (1997), fifteen Social Funds incorporated micro-financing activities into their other subsidized activities. It is worth observing that half of these Funds were

---

19 Micro-financing activities were born thanks to an initiative of specialized NGOs and commercial banks, such as the BRI-Unit Desa (Indonesia), the Grameen Bank (Bangladesh), K-Kep (Kenya) and Prodem/BancoSol (Bolivia). These establishments demonstrated that populations who are traditionally excluded from the formal financial sector can actually constitute a market for innovative and commercially-viable banking services. The establishments that usually succeed in this endeavor are mainly local organizations, commercially competitive and able to reach a large number of poor people, according to CGAP, 1998 : The World Bank Consultative Group for Assistance to the Poorest).

located in Latin America and Africa. There were only six of the Funds concerned at the time that directed 20 percent of funds from the World Bank to running micro-financing operations. This is a low figure, knowing that these small income and job-generating projects are one of the most efficient ways to create durable occupations. Nevertheless, the conclusions of this evaluation should be cited:

- The majority of Social Funds studied are not in a position to apply fully, or to impose the application of the rules expected of a micro-financing institution providing financial services to a very vulnerable group. The evaluation concludes this may not be their role;

- As a rule, the Funds cannot address the development of existing financial capacities or micro-financing institutions. Their role must be restricted to finding intermediaries for this task, as far as possible, regardless of the existing available channels with whom they may collaborate.

These conclusions sound rather categorical and inconsistent. Several studies carried out by the ILO around the same period reached just the opposite conclusions. For its part, the studies conducted under the Action Programme on Women's Participation in Social Funds considered that:

- Social Funds did not make loans directly but worked through intermediaries, such as village banks, NGOs or cooperatives;

- Credits were granted at the market rate in order to encourage better repayment, knowing that alternative credit sources were not advantageous. Repayments rates were excellent overall: in 1997, the repayment rate in the Social Funds of Chili (FOSIS), Honduras (FHIS), Guatemala (FIS) and Peru (FONCODES) ranged between 94 to 97 percent;

- Most borrowers were poorer than those who could obtain larger loans from commercial banks. Micro-financing operations were usually followed up by programmes of micro-enterprise development, based on training, transfer of technologies from developed to less-developed countries, marketing assistance and business administration.

In Latin America, micro-financing operations supported by the Social Funds had considerable success raising incomes, but much less impact on job-creation. This was not the case in Honduras where the 5 percent of Fund resources (Del Cid, 1997) allocated to this type of operation created 10 percent of permanents jobs attributable to the Fund. The Programme of Enterprise Development in the Egyptian Social Fund (Keir-El Din, 1997) generated in 1996 more than 60 percent of the permanent jobs owed to the Fund and over 55 percent of temporary jobs. Furthermore, this sub-programme was the forerunner of a nation-wide programme that was the first of its kind in Egypt. It also emerged from this example that nearly 40 percent of the applicants who benefitted from the loans from the Egyptian Social Fund were women. Moreover, 80 percent of the members of the Fund-assisted community banks are women.

This overview has shown that the Social Funds usually made rather limited use of micro-financing operations intended to promote income and job-creation. There were some successful exceptions, such as the large-scale involvement in the creation of durable jobs and in the promotion of women activities in Egypt. Bearing all this in mind, the conclusions made in the World Bank evaluation already mentioned and summarized below, can be questioned. This evaluation focused on the hypothesis that the Funds were not qualified to undertake this type of activities rather than on the results of these activities. Yet, this claim is challenged by the facts. Quite the contrary, it is possible to include within the development activities of the Funds the establishment of local credit institutions so that they can improve their performance. Finally, the few experiences of Social Funds in the field of micro-financing tend to confirm that they can efficiently remedy occasional deficiencies in this area. This does not mean that they must compete with these institutions when they do exist. It is regrettable there are so few activities related to micro-financing operations in the Social Funds, given the results obtained. This is all the more so since this activity can be replicated because all the financing from the Fund can be recycled. This can therefore be a good means of perpetuating the re-use of international loans or grants, which are not inexhaustible after all.

III.5   Development of local construction enterprises

As already mentioned, Social Funds rely on intermediaries to perform construction or rehabilitation works. These usually are small local enterprises and on occasion, NGOs or communities having the necessary skills. AGETIPs act as the delegated contract managers for the municipalities. In other words, municipalities commission them to recruit and supervise the local consulting firms and the small enterprises handling the works.

Social Funds, which intervene mainly in local destitute and remote zones, are often unable to find small enterprises and local consulting firms that can carry out proper tenders and perform the works according to specification. Social Funds encountered this problem from the outset and managed to tackle it only in the early nineties. At that time, under the influence of AGETIPs and the Malagasy Intervention Fund for Development[20], Social Funds started to adopt Operation Manuals as well as means that enabled the creation of small enterprises.

The experience of the Funds in Latin America has been uneven when it comes to the choice of intermediaries. Up to 1997, the operations of infrastructure building and rehabilitation in the Bolivian Fund (Contreras, 1997) were shared between the village communities and the enterprises at the rate of 30 and 70 percent respectively. It should be noted that these enterprises of various sizes were not necessarily local. In Honduras (Del Cid, 1997), the main infrastructure works representing 95 percent of activities within the Social Development Fund were performed by firms

---

20 The World Bank commissioned the ILO to design the FID in Madagascar and the Operation Manual..

and, to a lesser extent, by NGOs that met the necessary requirements. Many other Funds focused mainly on supplying various social services and relied on the local communities in the process. It appears that Latin American Funds did not create training activities that could benefit petty contractors, the local consulting firms or small local enterprises. Had they existed, these activities could have prepared them for the administration and contract management tasks on one hand, and the design and implementation using HIMO methods and local materials/equipment, on the other. This can partly explain the low impact of these Funds on employment, as the founders were concerned essentially with the purely social dimension of these institutions.

On the one hand, it is said that the extensive use of enterprises may lead to a loss of support from local communities for the maintenance and operation of the completed infrastructures. On the other, it is true that expecting ill-qualified community groups to supervise the work poses an even greater risk of sabotaging the projects. Ultimately, what is required is to provide appropriate training plans so that the beneficiaries can get involved in the various phases of the works, and become prepared enough to assume responsibility for the completed infrastructures.

In Africa, it was the AGETIPs that popularized the nearly systematic use of enterprises to carry out the works. However, these agencies had to deal with many obstacles, especially at the outset, because they often had not taken the necessary time to train these small enterprises. In spite of this fact, the impact of AGETIPs has been significant on the local construction industry, especially on small contractors and local consulting firms. Moreover, the example set by these agencies has encouraged other donors to set up similar methods.

It was within FASO BAARA, the AGETIP of Burkina Faso that several measures were taken in 1996 to limit the list of eligible enterprises, based on very stringent technical criteria. This measure facilitated their classification into different categories. These measures meant that their qualifications could be more clearly distinguished. A workshop jointly organized by the ILO and AFRICATIP in 1999 highlighted the needs for training within the AGETIPs. Consequently, the AGETIP of Senegal requested a special type of assistance to offer comprehensive training to the personnel of small enterprises and local consulting firms with whom it collaborates. This reveals how wide the gap is that needs to be bridged despite the efforts already made in many cases. Calling upon enterprises from the private sector is a good first step but bolstering their abilities, especially in HIMO techniques, remains an essential objective and is indispensable for their viability and survival. If the private sector approach is to be successful over time, two other factors must equally be present: competitive costs and high quality finished work.

Two Social Funds came to take a set of measures to facilitate not only the emergence but also the capacity-building of small local enterprises. The National Programme of Social Action (PNAS) in Rwanda, introduced in 1993, was remodelled after the war in 1994. Its objective was to help the country re-launch a set of economic and social activities based on the rehabilitation of small grass-roots infrastructures. It must be pointed out that the majority of small enterprises disappeared after the genocide, either because their staff was killed in the conflict or because their equipment was stolen. In order to reduce costs, between two and ten contracts at a time were signed with these local consulting firms. The Fund decided to help them reorganize; it commissioned them to design and carry out the infrastructure programmes. The PNAS also facilitated the creation of a network of new enterprises. Frame 9 summarizes the results.

Frame 9: **How the PNAS in Rwanda incited the construction of small construction enterprises after the 1994 conflict**

During the period that stretched from July 1995 to June 1998, the PNAS concluded 223 contracts worth nearly $10 million for very diverse infrastructure works with 112 small enterprises. The maximum number of contracts signed with any one enterprise was eight with the value of each contract not exceeding $45,000. In addition, 85 contracts were signed for the supply of school equipment. These contracts were divided among 49 enterprises, workshops and associations of carpenters for a total of nearly $1.17 million. The number of contracts by supplier was limited to five, with an average value of $13,500.

A total of 53 contracts, worth a total of $670,000 were concluded with 13 local consulting firms for the design and supervision of the works. Similarly, 61 contracts were concluded with eight NGOs who were to act as intermediaries for certain community-related activities. In order to reduce the costs, the contracts signed with these local consulting firms comprised between 2 and 10 projects. On average, 7.7% of the total budget went to design and supervision, which is a very reasonable figure. The emergence of these small enterprises was bolstered by training activities in the field of enterprise management and use of the appropriate construction technologies (buildings, rural access roads and water supply).

The development of small enterprises is an important activity in the Malagasy Fund, where training has played a vital role. A 1999 evaluation of this activity highlighted the positive effects which the Fund had produced in this field and which included:

- Increase the number of permanent staff employed by these enterprises;
- Substantial investment in the purchase of equipment needed to develop their capacity;
- Visible improvement in their management competence relative both to accounting and to working conditions;
- Extension of technical skills, particularly noticeable in the management of the building sites;
- Shift of certain enterprises from the informal to the formal sector, as soon as they were able to manage an accounting system and to respect both fiscal and labour legislation.

In spite of their progress, these enterprises remain fragile and have yet to overcome certain difficulties. These include irregular demand stemming from excess dependency on FID activities and continued difficulty obtaining bank loans owing to their unsteady situation.

It is instructive to examine the case of the Armenian Social Fund, launched in 1995. As of the second year, 10 to 15 small and medium-sized local enterprises submitted tenders for the implementation of almost 50 projects. After five years, nearly all of the 400 to 500 small construction enterprises in the country were in a position to participate.

At the same time, the Social Fund set up a training system relative to preparing tender documents. This training was offered during meetings held as pre-tender sessions. Gradually, the Social Fund in liaison with the communities organized the tendering process jointly. Note that it was the Social Fund that always retained the supervisory role in the contract awarding process. It further remained responsible for setting up a system of maintenance for building sites and for the payments for work completed. In this connection, about 250 small firms received training.

As a general rule, in order to develop a network of local consulting firms and small enterprises, it is important for Social Funds to be in a position to launch a whole series of activities, which can include as follows:

- to draft Operation Manuals in which the provisions for tendering favour the recruitment of local small enterprises;
- to organize training courses based on labour-intensive construction technologies;
- to establish a set of support measures to facilitate firms' access to micro-financing to purchase equipment;
- to institute procedures that allow timely payment for work in a number of installments; and
- to divide the work into small segments which fall more easily within the capacities of the preferred small enterprises.

It has been observed that these actions can lead to impressive results. Ignoring these principles, on the other hand, may have harmful consequences, such as when works are awarded to large enterprises outside the target area of the Fund. These firms are little inclined to create jobs and even less to recruit part of the labour force locally. It is noteworthy that many of the purposely designed policies that led to tangible results in certain Funds (Egypt, Madagascar, and Rwanda, among others) were set up with the support of the ILO. It is regrettable to note that the policies currently recommended in most of the Social Funds, including AGETIPs, do not stress enough the importance of the application of the above measures. They tend instead to award contracts to the lowest bidder without giving much thought to the development of the local construction industry, in other words, to the emergence and reinforcement of a network of competent SMEs throughout the country. Such a goal would obviously require the adoption of new measures, including different procedures for tendering from those currently used. It would also require implementation of a structuring programme for the sector with the support of the AGETIP. It is necessary to help to found professional associations of SMEs and local consulting firms and to develop their capacities. These associations could also dispense training programmes, offer insurance and mutual-guarantee schemes and help adopt uniform rules and standards in this sector.

This approach is already emerging in some AGETIP projects financed by international donors such as the KFW, the ACDI or the AFD. These donors accept procedures favoring the tender of the best bidder rather than the lowest bidder while also introducing training programmes more consistently. The KFW provided funding for training sessions within the FASO BAARA (AGETIP of Burkina Faso) and the NIGETIP. The KFW is currently the main source of funding for these two AGETIPs, ahead of the World Bank. It appears that the KFW uses a more pragmatic and comprehensive approach, aimed at obtaining results rather than imposing restrictive procedures. It is more inclined to accept the direct agreement procedures, or procedures founded on the selection of a restricted list for the designation of firms, unlike the World Bank. Apparently, there are fewer defaults and fewer cases of guardianship in KFW-funded projects than in those that are World Bank-funded.

CHAPTER **4**

Increasingly engaged beneficiaries

IV.1 Community participation

At their best, community organizations serve as transmitters for the promotion and development of local initiatives which is the very foundation of popular participation on the part of communities. These are highly diverse bodies: users associations of the same service, groups of producers, cooperatives, women groups, NGOs and even lobby groups defending their rights or interests (Ghai and Vivian, 1992). These bodies may be striving to defend farmers interests and develop relative autonomy, be strengthening their status in society and negotiating their rights, mainly with the regional administration. They may be the driving force in launching programmes for investment, training, savings and loans, for instance, and lobby diligently so that the services, works or infrastructure loans set up truly serve the populations concerned (Garnier, Majeres, 1992). Others, in contrast, connected to the local political and administrative authorities, will use those connections with the administration to obtain benefits or financing from cooperation agencies or NGOs, among others.

In this light, it is to be expected that Social Funds call upon the local communities and strive to make them the driving force behind their operations. Yet, it was only in the early nineties that the Funds were designed to offer the beneficiaries more substantial participation in project implementation and to engage them deeply in their operation and maintenance. This occurred because the first generation of Social Funds had pursued mainly short-term objectives and lacked the time to organize popular participation in their projects. As explained in Chapter

II, participation is organized mainly on two levels: a) under the Project Committees who represent the beneficiaries with the intermediaries; and b) through the internal procedures of the Social Funds that specify that beneficiaries must bear a certain percentage of costs. This percentage varies usually between 10 and 20 percent. The contribution can be made in cash, but more often takes the form of participation in works and in materials.

Unlike AGETIPs that operate mainly in urban or semi-urban areas, Social Funds can be geared more equally to the participation of beneficiary communities or groups, since they intervene mainly in rural environments. It is certainly easier to find homogenous groups who share the same concerns in rural settings. In contrast, urban areas require much larger and more elaborate projects, which surpass the capacities of local groups or associations. When it comes to participation, AGETIPs operate differently from Social Funds as the latter work mainly with municipalities.

Social Funds seek to engage the participation of beneficiaries mainly in order to set up an effective system to operate and maintain the completed works. It is far easier to marshal the support of the populations in perpetuating completed works once they have been consulted in both selecting and conducting the projects. It is a complex endeavor to engage the participation of beneficiaries, which requires building a broad consensus among the various parties represented. This consultation process takes place at a price in that it delays the implementation of an operation. Moreover, there are numerous participants, from the Funds' personnel to the beneficiaries and including the municipalities or different intermediaries involved. Several studies (World Bank, 1997 and Siri, 1998) concluded, however, that the benefits of community participation far outweigh the potential complications.

In Latin America, the participation of the community was sought more or less directly depending on the Funds. Yet, this process unfolded, it seems, independently of any given strategy. This can be explained by the difficulty, outlined earlier, of setting up a system with beneficiaries at the center of the development process while, at the same time, attempting to limit the risks of recovery by prominent citizens or politicians. In order to avoid this dilemna, some Social Funds[21] called upon the help of NGOs and confessional organizations for two purposes: to target the poorest segments of the population and to promote community initiatives, in accordance with general Fund objectives. In spite of these rare instances, the Inter-American Development Bank estimated in 1997 (Siri, 2000) that these intermediaries were involved on average in only 15 percent of Social Fund-sponsored projects. These organizations, apart from a few successful cases, cannot replace direct community participation for many reasons: they often have their own priorities; their budget does not always match their ambitions; their technical and operational capacity is often exaggerated; and, their area of intervention is often very limited. Several Funds, such as those in Chili (FOSIS), Peru (FONCODES) and Guatemala (FONAPAZ) used other means to encourage community participation by acting more globally to develop the institutional and administrative capacities of rural communities. For this purpose, custom-made training programmes were put into place.

In Africa, more recent Social Funds were specifically designed to integrate the participation of village communities, whose capacities, however, are still underdeveloped. To achieve this purpose, these Social Funds may intervene by means of three methods:

- By establishing Project Committees and defining their role;
- By requiring contributions from the communities that receive subsidies from a Social Fund; and,
- By dispensing training to teach a community how to manage and monitor project construction.

---

21 This is the case of Funds in Chili, Haiti, Panama and Bolivia (Siri, 2000).

In Frame 10, it is explained how Village Project Committees' action is organized in the Social Action Fund of Malawi, set up in 1997. This example is very illustrative of the terms and conditions required for the participation of a community benefitting from Fund actions.

Frame 10: **The tasks of Project Committees in the Malawi Social Action Fund (MASAF)**

Establishment of the participatory process: Organizing preliminary meetings in which the entire community is represented fairly; discussing priority needs; electing a Project Committee; possibly using the services of a representative of the local government administration, of an implementing agency or of a member of the community to act as an intermediary between the Project Committee and the Social Fund.

Level of community contribution: Normally, the community is asked to contribute up to 20 percent of the total cost of the project, either in equivalent work or by supplying locally available materials.

Management of expenses: Signing of an agreement between the Fund and the Project Committee; opening an account by the Project Committee and reception of funds in instalments, in step with the progress of works.

Implementation and monitoring of works: The Project Committee handles purchasing and hires small local contractors to perform the works. It supervises operations, reports on their progress to the Fund and monitors the proper handling of financial procedures adopted by common consent with the Fund. The beneficiaries are asked to assess the results of the project upon its completion.

Not only does the financial contribution of the beneficiaries deepen their sense of involvement in the works, but it also increases the number of projects that may be assisted by the Social Fund. Table 5 presents an overview of the percentage contribution of beneficiaries to some of the Social Funds in Africa.

Table 5: The contribution of beneficiaries to project costs in some Social Funds in Africa	
The Comores (FADC)	20 percent minimum for all types of project
Madagascar (FIDII)	10 percent for all projects and 20 percent for pilot projects directly managed by the communities
Malawi (MASAF)	20 percent for all projects
Rwanda (PNAS)	Given the extreme poverty of the communities caused by the 1994 war, no percentage has been set. However, since 1996, the only projects designated as priorities are those to which the communities are willing to contribute

These figures must be compared with the level of contribution asked of the municipalities, which usually does not exceed 5 percent in the case of AGETIPs. Moreover, mixed results have sprung from the collaboration between the AGETIPs and the communities. While the concept of decentralizing management responsibilities is new to Africa, the idea of assuming financial management is even newer. The managers or employees chosen from the administrations/municipalities lack experience and there is high turnover. This reduces the impact of training activities dispensed by the AGETIP. The links are often weaker between the AGETIP and community officials than those forged between the Social Fund and beneficiaries. Furthermore, officials from semi-urban communities are not nearly as close to the population they are supposed to represent as those in rural communities. All this explains why it is quite difficult to obtain the community's financial participation in AGETIPs. The NIGETIP agency asked only for 5 percent financial contribution before the start of works in the Urban Infrastructure Rehabilitation Project (PRI). The request, even for this modest amount, caused many delays in the projects, ranging from delayed payments to non-payment of contributions. For the second phase of the PRI, the method chosen consisted of separating the communities' contributions from the investments made by the NIGETIP.

The contribution of the populations is the least tangible in Central and Eastern Europe and in the countries of the ex-Soviet Union

(Goovaerts, 2000). In practice, Social Funds arrive to act as a substitute for communities having little structure or organization. Furthermore, in these countries, there are neither intermediaries nor a banking system flexible enough to handle the transactions needed between the Funds, the Project Committees and enterprises. The Social Funds in Armenia and Moldavia are the only ones in which a certain balance was achieved between local authorities and the real beneficiaries. The Moldavian Fund has the added advantage of stressing the institutional and managerial capacity-building of local communities so that they can become responsible partners, aware of beneficiaries' true interests.

Finally, the development of grass-roots associations is inseparable from that of decentralized communities. It would be hard to imagine a Project Committee drawn from local associations taking responsibility for a series of projects if these associations were not representative of the community or municipality concerned. This Committee must be able to cooperate and to counterbalance a local administration, which often has limited competence. In this context, the overall results of Social Funds able to work with these two bodies is, for the most part, positive and constantly improving.

IV.2 Enhanced decentralization

In terms of volume, the number of decentralized public jobs represents 12 to 25 percent of total public employment in OECD countries, against almost 8 percent in Asia and 2.5 percent in Africa. It must be pointed out that an effective decentralization process demands a long, costly and unpredictable transfer of some of the traditional tasks of the State to the regional administrations. Practically-speaking, decentralization should always involve a redistribution of resources and authority and a certain degree of delegation of decision-making and action. It offers, at least in theory, the opportunity to expand the autonomy of a community, to encourage popular participation in the day-to-day management of public affairs and to make better distribution of the Government resources (Jacobi, 1991). In practice, the scarcity of financial, technical and human resources of decentralized bodies in developing countries hinders them in performing their already heavy tasks collecting local taxes and duties, managing community services, recording civil status and managing State property, to mention but a few. The inertia observed at this level in certain countries, particularly in Africa, simply reflects burdens. In contrast to Latin America where decentralization is now a reality, it is only recently that Africa embarked on this process, often under pressure from international fund providers. Governments usually start this process with reluctance given their wide fear of losing political or economic ground. Reforms in local taxation systems drag on and the transfer of authority is not accompanied by a transfer of the corresponding resources.

In this difficult context, Social Funds are increasingly adapting their methods to cope with the presence or absence of decentralized administrations having adequate means. The first experiences aimed at involving local administrations in the operations of Funds can be found in Latin America, specifically in the Funds of Bolivia (FIS) and Honduras (FHIS). The approach consists of integrating the Fund activities into local development plans and to entrusting funds and direct responsibility for project implementation to these administrations. It further means creating a capacity-building programme for these administrations to manage and monitor projects, from the stage of tendering right through actual operation.

At the current stage, it is only a matter of recognizing this evolution in Social Funds, especially in Latin America. It is still important to ask how much significance to attach to this evolution. It would be unwise to consider decentralization a compulsory condition for every development project, which has been the tendency for some years now. In fact, decentralized administrations are still struggling in most regions where Social Funds can be found. This applies to the heavily centralized States of Central and Eastern Europe and countries of the ex-Soviet Union. Social Funds are definitely not intended as spearheads for the spread of decentralization. They can, however, become better coordinated, in theory, with an on-going decentralization process, just as they can support its advancement within the scope of specific objectives. In a recent report published by the World Bank (Parker and Serrano, 1999), it is proposed to adjust the design, and gradual transfer of responsibilities of a Social Fund, to the degree of decentralization reached in the host country. Such provisions are summarized in Table 6. It may still be too early to draw lessons from the experience of Funds that have worked with decentralized administrations. We can, nevertheless, cite some preliminary observations in this respect:

- On the one hand, there was a marked increase in the percentage of contribution to projects subsidized by the Funds whenever community investment plans existed. These plans reflect the real desire of local communities to identify the projects closest to their needs;

- On the other hand, decentralized administrations are tempted to distribute available resources equitably over their territory, sometimes to the detriment of real needs. This trend can be challenged by the influence of politicians and certain enterprises.

The above observations call for a word of caution. It is far too early to make any judgment on the role of Social Funds as regards decentralization. No doubt, time should do its work. We should do what is required to allow current experiences to unfold as practically as possible.

Table 6: Social Funds and decentralization

Country	Non decentralised	Partly decentralized	Fully decentralised
Characteristics of decentralization and of the local bodies (LB)	No effective local communities, no local budgets, lack of accounting	LB exist but have capacity constraints; a certain budget is already allocated to LB, improved accounting	Entirely capable LB, Budget autonomy, Proper accounting
Consequently ↓			
	1st Generation of Social Funds	2nd Generation of Social Funds	3rd Generation of Social Funds
Strategic objective	Social Funds as agents for change	Social Funds may promote fiscal decentralization	Social Funds help strengthen the tax system
Planning	Support to community projects	Support of community projects and those selected by the LB	Support of local development priorities
Financing	Mixed: (i) directly to the communities, and (ii) works supervision delegated by the Social Fund	Transition to credible LB with improved accounting	All funds are transferred to the LB
Award of contracts and procurement	Mixed: (i) community management of contracts; and, (ii) direct management of contracts by the Social Funds	Mixed: (i) community management of contracts; (ii) management of contracts directly by the LB; and, (iii) management of some contracts also by the Social Fund	Management of all the contracts concluded by the LB and the communities
Strategy for shifting from one SF to another type of SF	LB set up to pass to the 2nd generation of SF	Functional LB to pass to the 3rd generation of SF	SF resources are linked to the tax system

IV.3 Sustainability

A long-standing issue involves post-project operation and maintenance. Albert Hirschman drew attention to the lack of maintenance as early as 1964: "That may be one of the weak points that characterizes developing countries and permeates all spheres of economy," he said. "...eroding soils, trucks that break down, leaking roofs, machines beyond repair prematurely, swaying bridges and clogged irrigation canals are all symptoms of one overall and puzzling fact: the absence of maintenance for existing capital in poor countries". This question remains highly   relevant almost forty years later. Rare are the projects currently being designed in developing countries that make sufficient provision for vital institutional and budgetary support and training of users, both of which are prerequisites for operating and maintaining completed works.

Obviously, this statement also applies to Social Funds and AGETIPs. A whole series of measures is being included in Funds to ensure greater project sustainability. It is necessary to remain wary, however, even if the several reforms underway, especially in Africa, are likely to benefit directly the operation and maintenance of projects typically subsidized by Social Funds. These institutions are involved in one way or another in the process of reform whether this might be: a transfer of authority accompanying administrative decentralization; a reform of the local tax system; or the set-up of a Road Maintenance Fund. This is a highly complex matter, which must be approached on a broader and more elaborate scale. The recurrent budgets for the operation and maintenance must be discussed as early as the stage of feasibility studies between the Project Committees, local communities and the decentralized administrations. This issue is equally crucial for Social Funds and AGETIPs, with possibly a slight advantage for Latin America, Central and Eastern Europe and the ex-Soviet Union, where maintenance matters have received somewhat greater attention than in Africa.

It comes as no surprise then that Social Funds and AGETIPs

gradually introduced a series of measures to ensure the sustainability of subsidized projects. It can be said that:

- Social Funds must finance only projects that meet three criteria so as to extend their life to the maximum, namely: (1) the project must be a real priority for the community, who must be willing to contribute substantially to it in kind or in financial resources; (2) the technical provisions must be compatible with the local operation and maintenance capacities; and, (3) strict measures must be taken to guarantee the subsequent operation of the project;

- The various types of infrastructures built should be described in a small Owner Manual, intended for the owners or the users' associations. This Manual must specify the terms, conditions, frequency of maintenance, details of operation, the origin and budgeting of the needed financial resources in addition to the institutional characteristics of the project;

- Users must receive training at the time of construction.

Even with the aid of these measures, Funds are continuously confronted with a highly complex problem. They must, therefore, keep close watch over the projects even years after they have become operational. There are many reasons to justify this vigilance, the most important of which include:

- The flaws in technical design, sometimes due to the inexperience of the recent local consulting firms. The problem might be over-sized concrete-based works, which increases costs, or the under-sized drainage works, resulting in rapid deterioration. These conclusions are regularly drawn in the evaluation reports or the technical audits required by the World Bank;

- The traditional assumption that the responsibility of the operation and maintenance belongs to the central administration, even when it is incapable of doing so. The beneficiaries do not always fully understand the increasingly regular transfer of these responsibilities to local bodies, communities and even to the users;

■ The fact that Social Funds and the providers of funds still tend to underestimate the costs and difficulties of operation and maintenance. They assume this is the minimum contribution to be expected from the users, in return for external contributions. In practice, they are not sufficiently objective when assessing the actual technical, human and financial capacities of participants;

■ The high cost of regular maintenance of certain infrastructures, such as rural access roads. This cost may represent up to 50 percent of the initial cost after five years. Regular maintenance can usually be handled locally by use of a system of fees compatible with users' resources (D'Hont and van Imschoot, 1999)[22]. This is not true for systematic periodic maintenance that must come from budgetary provisions within special maintenance funds, managed and funded by the designated regional or local administrations.

Projects developed with the support of AGETIPs are usually larger than those subsidized by Social Funds. The former depend entirely on the financial capacities of the municipalities for their subsequent operation and maintenance. The AFRICATIP network acknowledged, as of 1997 (World Bank, April 1997), that the lack of necessary measures to ensure maintenance constituted a weakness within these agencies. To deal with such problems, the municipalities enjoying support from the AGETIP must establish priority investment and maintenance plans, entirely managed with the beneficiaries. The already complex maintenance issue is further complicated by the fact that AGETIPs normally intervene only during implementation. It is necessary to make a start by providing greater assistance and training to the communities, both prior to and especially after implementation. Several AGETIPs and Social Funds

---

22 In 1999, two writers made an evaluation of standard maintenance operations entrusted to communities that border rural rural access roads in Madagascar. These were rural access roads rehabilitated under the FIFAMANOR project in the region of Vakinankaratra with the support of the ILO/NORAD. Maintenance of these rural access roads in good condition is considered vital by the communities and the beneficiary populations for the economic and social development of their region. There has been a promising increase in the community's commitment This is exemplified by the erecting of toll booths, by a contribution from the community budget and by occasional voluntary community maintenance work.

currently have an Owner Manual already mentioned for each completed infrastructure. This Manual describes the necessary maintenance activities and calculates the recurrent budget required. Despite the adoption of these measures, communities are often short of the needed financial resources. AGETIPs have tried to find the start of a solution to this problem in two ways:

- By promoting the construction of economic infrastructures, such as markets, bus stations, shops and sanitary facilities. These activities generate an income that municipalities can set aside for the maintenance of infrastructures;

- By introducing the concept of free management, which consists of helping communities delegate management contracts for these economic infrastructures to the private sector by using tenders. Thus, management is awarded to the best bidder or to the one who offers the most advantageous financial terms as well as the best occupational safety and health conditions.

The above cited evaluation made by the World Bank in 1997 of 51 Social Funds spread over 34 countries also examined the sustainability of the different types of basic infrastructures. The evaluation divided the projects into three categories and cautiously concluded that:

- The projects designed to provide social services (mainly schools and care centers) usually deliver the expected services. This achievement rests on the fact that these projects call upon communities' participation and that beneficiaries feel very concerned by this type of service. These projects are usually well-designed and are jointly planned with the corresponding administrations;

- It is more difficult to evaluate the capacity of economic and micro-financing infrastructure projects to offer the services anticipated. This somewhat mixed conclusion results from the lack of attention to operation and maintenance questions at the design stage. Such weaknesses are exarcerbated by the lack of commitment of beneficiaries or users and the relevant administrations.

It is too early to assess the sustainability of operations within the Social Funds in Central and Eastern Europe and in the ex-Soviet Union over the past few years. There are some indications, however, that most of the above conclusions apply to this part of the world also (Goovaerts, 2000). The maintenance/operation tandem is also neglected in these regions, right from the stage of the feasibility studies through the training of users and essential recurrent budgets.

The operation and maintenance of projects remains the weakest facet of development projects in the least developed countries. It is hardly conceivable that most local administrations repeatedly devote so little concern or adequate means to the maintenance and operation of development projects funded by foreign aid. This is even more unfortunate since these projects are part of the State's Public Investment Programme. International donors are increasingly refusing to fund new investments unless local governments solemnly commit to providing the recurrent budgets and maintenance systems. This issue is becoming more complex because existing systems must be decentralized. Local administrations must engage directly with the beneficiary communities. The current strategy of the Governments and fund providers is to involve local participants to the maximum in assuming the responsibility for the projects intended for them. Social Funds are unquestionably in a better position than AGETIPs to uphold this strategy. There is little doubt that the amount of time and means of action required generally continue to be underestimated.

CHAPTER 5

Dimension of Social Funds and evaluation of their impact

V.1   Macro-economic dimension of Social Funds

In countries where Social Funds have been established, social policies, in the conventional sense[23], are still in their infancy. This is also the case for economies in transition in Central and Eastern Europe where the social planning of the Soviet era has come nowhere near to being replaced by more flexible and better-adapted social policies. This comes as no surprise when we see industrialized countries enjoying advanced social policies allocate 35 to 40 percent of the Government's budget to redistribution! Obviously, the establishment and development of a social protection policy, in which Social Funds and other programmes stand as important pillars, is an attractive alternative for many emerging economies. However, these Funds must exist on a large enough scale to offer underprivileged groups even limited access to basic social services. It should be recalled that current Social Funds are being designed to serve as development instruments at grass-roots level, and not solely as compensatory measures. They now provide social services and income rather than operating as simple systems of redistribution. The question is then to know to what extent the dimension of a Social Fund determines its contribution to social development?

Before elaborating on this question, it is necessary to draw a parallel with the set up of large-scale public works programmes, initially devised as ad hoc instruments to fight unemployment and extreme poverty. This

---

23 In other words, fighting poverty by redistribution and mitigating the negative effects of economic policies by supplying social services to a maximum number of people. Léon Walras discussed this aspect in terms of social economy, the theory of social distribution between individuals in a society.

type of intervention, based on Keynes's "investment multiplier," was first used by industrialized countries, including the United States[24], in the thirties. Since the sixties, these programmes have multiplied in developing countries (Costa and Mouly, 1974) with W.A. Lewis and R. Nurske as their main advocates and theoreticians. Despite the large number of programmes that succumbed to the test of time and the strict requirements of international aid, many of these programmes continue to contribute quite effectively to poverty alleviation. These include the Promotion Nationale in Morocco and the Jawahar Rojgar Yojna in India, which are usually well-integrated into the development strategies of the country. Among other benefits, they contribute substantially to job-creation[25]. These programmes avoided the frequent traps often mentioned in explanations of the failures of large public works programmes including: insufficient use of HIMO methods, preference for short-term job-creation, the inadequate size of programmes and excess reliance on external financing.

In practice, several restrictions prevent adopting the macro-economic dimension needed in these programmes. There is, for instance, a scarcity of managers with adequate skills assigned to these programmes. Political priorities have not reflected the importance of the stakes involved. Moreover, funding rests too heavily on international aid for there to be any real attempt to make improvements. In addition, inflation remains a serious underlying threat in developing countries, where monetary creation must be wisely iimplemented. Finally, even if it were possible to determine the ideal dimension of a programme, the difficulty of evaluating its real economic and social benefits would limit its usefulness. The ex-post global analysis of shadow prices has always been a tricky and controversial subject.

Between 1959 and 1969, the annual budget of Chantiers de Lutte contre le Sous-développement in Tunisia rose to 2.4 percent of GNP. This is a unique case since the majority of national large-scale programmes

---

24 The Works Administration Program (1933-40) created 13.7 million of years of work during its
7 years of existence.
25 In this way, the Indian program created every year around 1 billion work days!

that did take off, rarely exceeded 0.5 to 1 percent of GNP. Taking into account the above difficulties, this figure can be considered a realistic one. It is, however, the fruit of a genuine pro-active policy in favour of income and job-creation, and of poverty alleviation in a given country.

Even with all these limitations, the reasoning behind such programmes is no longer seriously challenged when they are well-designed (Abedian, 1993 and Subbarao,1997). Abedian claims, in referring to the case of South Africa, that economic growth is an indispensable yet insufficient condition for reducing poverty. A national programme of public works serving as a special instrument of redistribution would help stabilize the economy while encouraging growth. To this end, such a programme should stimulate job and income-intensive projects and focus on training the participants and promoting the creation of infrastructures. For his part, Subbarao pointed out the qualities of these programmes for the task of poverty alleviation, based on his examination of several samples of large-scale programmes operating in Africa, Latin America and Asia since 1987. He hoped, however, that these operations would insist more firmly on the participation of women and that of the private sector and that they would facilitate the true involvement of the poorest.

What is the situation of Social Funds in this perspective? Several countries have chosen this model to deal with sudden crises. They also chose it as a long-term instrument to fight unemployment and poverty. If we exclude the role of fund providers, it is difficult to pinpoint the reasons that incite a country to choose one type of programme over another. Countries with a more structured administration and a centralized tradition will certainly be more inclined to launch large-scale programmes of public works. This is true of India whose widely implanted territorial administration[26] was well adapted to such programmes. It must be acknowledged that the local level of public services in many developing countries do not usually have adequate human and financial resources, despite the increased decentralization of

---

26 The Indian Administration Service (IAS).

the past ten years. Consequently, Social Funds and AGETIPs are rapid and efficient alternatives to adopt in order to meet the needs of the poor and marginalized populations. In this respect, the case of Morocco offers a remarkable example. It is only recently that this country decided to strengthen the Promotion Nationale by creating a Social Development Agency, i.e. a Social Fund. Even if it is decentralized, the Promotion Nationale finances infrastructure projects chosen at the provincial level and conducted by HIMO methods, although it calls relatively little on community participation. While it operates on a regular budget, its resources may be increased for exceptional reasons, such as drought. In contrast, the mission of the Agency created in 2000 is to identify and finance projects urgently needed by the completely destitute.

In practice, the dimension of Social Funds remains comparable to that of large-scale programmes of public works. Their size reaches hardly beyond 0.5 percent of GNP in countries in Latin America and in Central and Eastern Europe. This leads many observers to wonder about the real impact of Social Funds. A study (Bigio, 1997)[27] by the Inter-American Development Bank (IDB) deemed the macro-economic impact of Social Funds uncertain despite the vast resources allocated by the World Bank and the IDB. The Fund in Nicaragua is the only one that has annual resources equivalent to 1 percent of GDP. Bigio concluded that the impact of these Funds would certainly be minimal given their modest size! He forgot, however, that the mandate of a Social Fund is to subsidize a large programme of small-size projects geared to the possibilities of the target groups. He also underestimated the intricacy of management problems that arise when conducting numerous small projects of different types. This complexity, usually a matter of insufficient capacities, inevitably restricts the possible dimension of these institutions.

It is thus impossible to assert that a Social Fund will have only marginal consequences if its annual disbursement capacity is below 1 percent of GNP. Previous experiences have revealed that, with few

---

27 Bigio G., refer to the article on the Inter-American Development Bank Study of Social Funds, p. 43-49.

exceptions, both types of institution, whether Social Funds or large programmes of public works, present comparable dimensions. These programmes cannot be expected to produce a substantial macro-economic impact if they are taken independently of one another. However, the macro-economic impact of several programmes of this type in the same country would be considerable if taken as a whole. The positive results of a study of this type conducted in Madagascar (Razafindrakoto, 1999) were cited above in paragraph 3.2.

What does stand out is the exceptional dimension of the Social Fund (FISE) in Nicaragua. The annual resources of this Fund surpass 1 percent of GNP. Frame 11 illustrates with figures the singularity of the FISE. It should be noted that no study has been made to measure the macro-economic impact of this Social Fund.

Frame 11: The size and main characteristics of the FISE of Nicaragua

The management of the FISE collaborates closely with the Ministries of Education and Health, the National Institute of Water and the Institute of Municipal Development. It has become the largest and most efficient institution for small economic and social infrastructure works. With yearly disbursements of up to $30-$35 million, the expenses of the FISE represent 20 percent of all public investments in Nicaragua and more than 60 percent of those in the social sector.

The FISE has updated its poverty map to improve the quality of its targeting efforts. The financial resources allocated to extremely poor municipalities amount to 57 percent of funding compared to 20 percent previously. Poor municipalities receive 36 percent of resources instead of 57 percent. As for municipalities that are not as poor, they receive only 7 percent of financing, compared with 23 percent previously.

Source: Project Appraisal Document, Third Social Investment Project, World Bank, October 1998.

V.2   Spill over effects

It has been shown that Social Funds have enjoyed a measure of success in integrating an entire set of principles and procedures, which make for their originality. For example, they combine multi-sector activities that are governed by identical operational rules within a completely autonomous institution. They also concentrate on funding projects that are identified as priorities by the communities themselves. Finally, they have a reputation for transparency, which contributes to their popularity with donors. It comes as no surprise then that by their very example, they act as a driving force and an incentive in their environment, even if the results are hard to measure. In this fashion, the Funds coordinate and enable the following bodies to work together:

- The different grass-roots associations, such as users' associations, women's associations, etc.;

- The most common intermediaries, such as NGOs or mutual credit institutions;

- The Government administration, whether the technical ministries or the decentralized services where they exist; and,

- The local SMEs, local consulting firms and other small contractors.

The synergy produced by this collaboration between parties opens the door to using participatory approaches, to improving the mobilization of local resources, to using strict procedures for tenders in the private sector, and to transferring responsibility for contract management to communities.

The Funds often support the efforts of various countries to decentralize the Government apparatus and to transfer responsibilities to the smallest municipalities and rural communities. They work to involve decentralized administrations in project selection and monitoring. Many such examples can be cited in Latin America, where decentralization is more advanced. The Funds in Bolivia (FIS), Chili (FOSIS) and Honduras (FHIS) are note-worthy (Siri, 2000) from this standpoint.

It is Goovaerts (2000) who mentions the Social Funds in Armenia, Moldavia and Tajikistan, where local authorities recognized the soundness of the Funds' contracting procedures, as introduced in the Operation Manuals. These methods are now applied to other investments administered by local communities. Goovaerts further noted that in these cases, civil society participates more willingly in the operation of schools, health centers and water projects.

It was also found that the Funds triggered or facilitated the revival of small and medium-size constructions firms in their command area. These firms are domiciled locally and comprise consulting firms, transporters and producers or suppliers of locally-made materials and equipment. The volume of investment generated by projects financed by the Funds serves to revive and develop these small enterprises. In turn, they incite the creation of small trade, local markets, and various small crafts and stands. This effect was documented in rural areas where the Malagasy FID has cooperated since 1993. Similar results were also recorded for the Funds in Armenia (ASIF) and Ethiopia (ESRDF). These projects, financed by the Social Funds in these two countries, gave municipalities experience in implementing projects useful to their needs. It also increased their capacity as Client to manage tenders and contracts with small companies suited to conducting HIMO works.

It is thanks to the financing of a Social Fund that certain activities once abandoned have fortunately reappeared in rural communities and spurred the impetus of the local community for its own development. The Social Development Fund (SDF) in Yemen has subsidized the rehabilitation of public cisterns in districts that depend mainly on the collection of rainwater to supply their villages. This water is used either for household tasks or for livestock. It is important to know that Yemen is an arid land suffering from chronic shortages of drinking water as well as depletion of its ground water. This depletion stems from excessive mechanical pumping that outstrip the capacities for replenishment of ground water. Several of the villages affected chose to continue the experiment and develop it further even after the initial subsidy was granted by the SDF. Local small contractors were called upon for this purpose, while Village Committees assumed the management of the small contracts themselves.

Most countries with a Social Fund or an AGETIP see a steady

reduction in unit prices, an improved quality in services and shorter completion times for the work. There are usually many reasons for this recovery in the construction market. For instance, the tender procedures employed lead to the creation of real competition between firms. The same applies to more timely payment procedures. Broadly-speaking, the confidence instilled between the Social Fund/AGETIP and small local contractors and other petty contractors and artisans acts as an encouragement to business. Amazing results emerged from a comparative study conducted in Yemen in 1997. The study involved primary schools all having the same dimensions and specifications, but built by different agencies or administrations. The results of this survey are presented in Table 7.

Table 7: Comparing the unit costs of primary school construction in Yemen				
Ministry of Education using its own funds	Implementation agency within the Ministry of Education*	Agency outside the Ministry of Education*	Public Works Programme (highly autonomous)**	SFD (autonomous management)**
477$/m2	278$/m2	197$/m2	160$/m2	150$/m2

* Sector-based projects set up by the World Bank

** Largely autonomous, multi-sector World Bank-led projects.

The technical ministries used to hold a virtual monopoly on construction conducted by public works departments before Social Funds or AGETIPs were set up in the country. The practices of these ministries had to evolve in order to offer comparable costs, given the competition waged by these more autonomous and effective institutions. This effect became discernible with the gradual disappearance of works performed by public works departments, including maintenance.

V.3   Evaluation of Funds and projects

It was not until the nineties, when Social Funds started to become development instruments, that more comprehensive ex-ante evaluations started to appear to prove their justification. Up until then, the temporary nature of the programmes accounted for the rather simple projections of the number of jobs expected in the short term and of their cost. Gradually, the World Bank used the various methods at its disposal to justify the creation of a Fund. The Bank further acknowledged that simple economic analyses were not sufficient to evaluate the anticipated impact of a Social Fund. Therefore, in addition to its standard methods for assessing the validity of a large-scale project, the World Bank focused on gathering information on a whole range of issues more specific to Social Funds. These topics included: the consistency of projects with the policies and standards of the administrations concerned; the establishment of viable operating systems; assessment of the main risks; and the designation of the most vulnerable groups. The economic and social validity of the Funds created over the past ten years, usually on the Bank's initiative, has not been challenged.

Social Funds are usually the object of ex ante analyses. Given their clear social orientation, these analyses include the following tools to varying degrees: social indicators, unit prices, a calculation of recurrent costs and an estimation of the genuine commitment of beneficiaries. More conventional methods of economic analysis are used when it comes to more productive projects. A 1998 study by Pérez de Castillo concluded that Funds usually applied social and economic evaluation methods well-adapted to their project portfolios. The majority of Funds include criteria for project eligibility often developed in the Operation Manuals. These criteria facilitate an initial judgment on all projects submitted. According to de Castillo, the choice of methodology and its complexity depends largely on the resources, technical capacities and time available.

The most important efforts in recent years were made in the area of ex post analyses of project impact. This type of analysis rests on two elements depending on whether the focus is the overall impact of a Fund, that of a project or even that of a set of projects in a specific sector.

Starting in 1989, the World Bank undertook evaluations of Social Funds from the standpoint of beneficiaries. It considered rightly that the opinion of beneficiaries was a crucial factor, since the Funds were institutions that monitored the needs of the populations. In this respect, let us recall a survey conducted in 1998 on eight Funds (Owen, Van Doemelen, 1998) that had undergone this type of evaluation in the course of 1989-1996. The study pointed up the need to have a better understanding of the contribution of the projects in improving the living conditions of poor populations with respect to water supply, to drainage systems, community clinics and schools. Another comprehensive evaluation of all Social Funds was conducted in 1997[28] by the World Bank, assisted by a large task force. Its aim was to highlight the strong points of many Social Funds so as to make better use of these in the design of future Funds. This thorough evaluation, which included surveys, experts' judgments and analyses, stands as a reference in the field.

Despite their success and their importance, there has been little reliable information until recently as to the direct impact of the projects within Social Funds on beneficiary households and on the services provided. To bridge this data gap, in 1998 the World Bank launched (Rawlings and al) an important impact study covering six countries. The four main objectives were as follows: 1) to determine the ability of these institutions to target poor populations; 2) to assess their impact on the living standards of the poor; 3) to evaluate their long-term viability; and, 4) to calculate their cost-efficiency ratio. The study encompassed the Social Funds in Armenia, Bolivia, Honduras, Nicaragua, Peru and Zambia. Table 8 provides the results of this study with regard to water supply, for instance. This Table gives an idea of the degree of detail

---

28 It is the Portfolio Improvement Program study: Review of the Social Funds Portfolio. The introductory paragraph of the conclusion states that Social Funds have important potential as an instrument of community development for the sustainable provision of services that benefit poor groups.

obtained. Similar tables are available which pertain to targeting the poorest, provision of health services and education, popular participation and the cost-efficiency ratio. It is essential to stress the statistical nature of this survey, hence the reliability of its results.

Table 8: Impact of a sample of Social Funds providing water supply		
Quality of services infrastructures		**Water available in the Social Fund projects**
	Nicaragua	25 days/month on average compared with 18 for outside Fund projects
	Honduras	At desired levels in 50 % of Fund projects, comp. with 21 % in other projects
	Bolivia	With a 4-10 percent increase in frequency
	Bolivia	Water quality: after training, the Social Fund projects have reduced faecal contamination from 55% to 13%
Use of water		**Net increase in water supply in the Social Fund projects in relation to the control group**
	Honduras	5%
	Bolivia	10% in Chaco, 18% in Resto Rural
	Nicaragua	25%
		Reduction in the time and distance to obtain water
	Honduras	42 minutes per month
	Bolivia	154 meters in Chaco, 55 meters in Resto Rural
	Nicaragua	600 meters
Impact on health		**Effects of water supply investments in Social Funds**
	Bolivia	Reduction in the duration of diarrhea and in the mortality of children under 5 years of age
	Nicaragua	A 14 to 25 % reduction in the incidence of stunting in children under 5 years of age
	Honduras	No impact detected on the incidence of diarrhea

Source: "Social Funds: Accomplishments and Aspirations", Proceedings of the Second International Conference on Social Funds, June 5-7, 2000, World Bank Institute, edited by A. Levine.

This statistical survey puts forward convincing evidence on the capacity of Funds to reach the target groups and improve their living conditions. Few development programmes can prove their effectiveness with the same degree of reliability. As mentioned earlier, it is a matter of growing interest to promoters of Social Funds to learn what specific results Social Funds deliver to benefit the poorest groups. This study, coordinated by the World Bank (Rawlings and al), was the first truly reliable attempt to evaluate the impact of Funds on the provision of basic social services to the poorest.

CHAPTER **6**

Bolstering priority fields
of action

Social Funds and AGETIPs have evolved extensively over the past few years and have been able to draw successfully on the experiences of Funds of the first generation. Many efforts have been undertaken in areas where the action of the Social Funds was insufficient. They focused on improving the designation of target groups and of satisfying women's aspirations, and on involving grass-roots associations and local communities more closely in all phases of project development. The Funds have recognized the even greater importance of the sustainability of their actions.

This chapter examines other vital elements that could be very useful within Social Funds and that could improve their performances. Some of the specific tools developed by the ILO in recent years will be discussed below. These tools could definitely be more widely deployed within the Social funds and AGETIPs.

VI. 1   Planning better the needs of local communities

Thanks to information campaigns launched by Social Funds or to the emulation of examples set by a neighboring village, communities become able to recognize what sort of projects are eligible ones, which grants they may obtain and the conditions under which this can be done. This explains why the Funds receive a substantial number of requests every year. A written application must first be submitted to the Fund, in accordance with the regulations in the Operation Manuals. The Fund then proceeds to an initial evaluation corresponding to the criteria. Once the proposal has been retained, a technical and socio-economic feasibility study is conducted, which is usually subcontracted to local consulting firms or individual consultants. It is at this stage that the request is examined to determine if it genuinely meets the needs of the community and if it falls within the Government's sector policy. Moreover, it must be ensured that the community commands the determination and skills needed to guarantee the subsequent maintenance and operation of the infrastructure or services in question. It must also be learned if the applicant can implement the project on its own or requires special training and how much it can contribute to the financing.

Given the large number of requests, the technical managers of the Fund do not have time to set up a detailed inventory of the infrastructures and services needed in the villages or zones concerned. Such a document would, however, be the ideal tool because it would ensure consistency and help to classify the priorities of a small region. Nevertheless, the quick evaluations made by Social Funds strive to correct distortions/interference usually coming from outside factors. Such interference may result when businessmen or prominent citizens attempt to reap political profits from a project. It is never easy to prevent collusion from taking place between a politician, a local community and an enterprise (Parker, Serrano, 1999). Broadly-speaking, these evaluation methods have enabled Funds to confirm the eligibility of projects proposed by the communities and to shift quickly into action, thus reinforcing their credibility. This realistic approach should be compared with other studies conducted in a specific environment using a process of consultation with the potential beneficiaries, in order to design an integrated development programme. Unfortunately, the village communities are often disappointed by this highly perfectionist approach. It rarely succeeds simply because the financing was not secured during the preliminary studies and in the end, the funds were never raised. Consequently, the pragmatism governing Social Funds has been appreciated by potential beneficiaries, who realize that the operations are selected and conducted with satisfactory deadlines and conditions.

Social Funds in Bolivia and Honduras finance only requests already included in the local investment plans. AGETIPs in Africa have adopted this approach for many years. Moreover, AGETIPs sometimes ask local consulting firms to draw up the urban priority plan for investments. These plans are later approved by the Municipal Councils. The list of priority projects are then submitted to a Municipal Development Agency or a Local Endorsement Committee. These groups are made up of representatives from the municipalities or key ministries, such as the Ministry of Local Affairs or the Ministry of Economy and Finance. The task of Social Funds or the AGETIPs is to ensure that village groups or the district associations are involved in the preparation of the plans. This participatory process varies widely from one country to another. It has also been observed that the local consulting firms are not always willing to incorporate the impact of the infrastructures and services proposed on employment. Yet, it is precisely this effect which has become increasingly attractive to local communities, who have to deal with the stark realities of underemployment or unemployment. Moreover, when projects in the rural environment are evaluated, it is important to examine how the poorest people in a community will benefit from the infrastructures or services proposed.

In recent years, The ILO has developed a system of Integrated Rural Accessibility Planning (IRAP)[29]. This tool facilitates data collection on infrastructure and services in terms of their location, condition and availability to the population. It also facilitates the process of choosing priorities and investments, as well as the identification of interventions with a view to improving their availability. The IRAP system also emphasizes capacity-building and the use of local materials and human resources to implement and maintain community projects. It links the use of appropriate technologies and labour-intensive methods. As a multi-sectoral instrument for integrated planning, the IRAP addresses the main issues affecting rural households in order to satisfy their vital

---

29 Refer to the Guide on Integrated Rural Accessibility Planning on Malawi, which is also of more general interest. This document was published in June 2000 by the ILO/ASIST Programme.

socio-economic needs. Frame 12 presents the case of Laos where this system has been employed.

Frame 12: **UNDP/ILO integrated planning project for access to basic services and infrastructures in Laos**

Laos is a small, under-populated and inaccessible land (4.5 million inhabitants). It is mainly mountainous, and bordered by Cambodia, Vietnam, China, Myanmar and Thailand. The density of the population is low with an average of 18 people for every km2 and some of the lowest incomes in Asia. The majority of people in rural areas live from agriculture of self-subsistence. The Government decided at one point to set up a participatory process of community development planning. This process was aimed at improving living conditions in rural areas and fighting poverty more effectively.

This IRAP-type project operates at provincial and district levels in order to: introduce and strengthen community-participation procedures, collect data, establish maps, build and maintain rural roads, and set priorities for project implementation. For these purposes, training programmes are organized over an 18-month period to enable the personnel of the communes and decentralized administrations to acquire skills in these areas.

This planning method helps identify priority actions in terms of transport (infrastructures and means or transport services) and to locate basic services. This project currently serves as a reference for the Government of Laos, which has created a Rural Development Committee in charge of broader implementation of these procedures. Other providers of funds such as NORAD or Sweden now use the IRAP approach as a tool to develop projects in rural areas. It should be mentioned that this approach was gradually developed by the ILO in collaboration with the World Bank on the basis of studies conducted in some African countries during the nineties. In addition to Laos, this approach is widely used in Asia, specifically in Cambodia and Indonesia, and throughout the Philippines as part of the decentralization strategy conducted by the Government there.

Local consulting firms and individual consultants who devise priority investment plans within Social Funds can be trained to use this approach, which has started to provide results and could be adapted to this context.

VI.2   Increasing the share of productive projects and employment creation

The data on Social Funds reveals that they finance a larger number of social projects and far fewer productive investments and income-generating activities or micro-financing projects. Two main reasons account for this situation. First, it should be recalled that beneficiary populations request social projects first (schools, health centers and water supply). This type of project can be carried out quite quickly. Moreover, there are various hindrances that considerably delay the construction of more productive projects, especially in a Fund's early days. These productive projects include micro-irrigation schemes, rural markets, economic infrastructures, income-generating activities and micro-financing operations. Consequently:

- Only part of the local community benefits from this type of projects, a problem usually linked to real estate issues (irrigation schemes);
- The technical studies for productive projects are usually more complex and demand more time, especially at the preparation and launching stages;
- There are very few intermediaries who can set up micro-credit operations; and,
- The matching contribution required for certain productive projects is often high and obtaining it demands much time and efforts.

The following example demonstrates this situation. Phase I of the Social Fund for Development in Yemen (SFD), in operation from mid-1997 to 2000[30], contained a preponderance of social infrastructures. These infrastructures represented 76 percent of the disbursements compared with 13 percent for other types of infrastructures, 3 percent for social services, 6 percent for income-generating activities and 2 percent

---

30 Newsletter of the Social Fund for Development in Yemen, No. 11, July-September 2000.

for capacity-building operations. The following reasons serve to elucidate
the high percentage of social infrastructures:

- The strong demand for rural schools in a country that is particularly
  under- equipped in this area[31];

- The critical scarcity of water in Yemen, which explains the high
  demand for water supply projects;

- The absence of mutual financial institutions to which micro-financing
  activities could be conferred. Furthermore, banks are not prepared to
  finance SMEs due to the risks involved, the small size of the market
  and current economic stagnation;

- The low capacity of NGOs in this country.

- Yemen's craftsmen are known for their competence in the area of
  low-cost quality construction. This definitely facilitates the
  construction of social infrastructures.

To counteract this unbalance, the SFD launched pilot-projects for
micro-financing and income-generating activities. It also focused on
training intermediaries and consultants to facilitate the set up of projects
that create more lasting jobs. The FID in Madagascar witnessed the same
evolution. Productive and economic projects made up 47 percent of the
funding in the second phase.

These examples represent the growing range of Social Funds that
must simply be given time to develop the capacities of intermediaries.
This evolution is natural and must be respected. Indeed, it should be
recalled that credibility of Funds is ensured from the outset of operation
by their rapid implementation of social investments for needy
populations. In logical order, it can be understood that a Social Fund
gives top priority to social projects and, then proceeds to plan for
satisfying local needs. This effort must strike a balance between the
various types of activities without overlooking the fact that the focus must
always remain on the most vulnerable.

---

31 Yemen has the lowest rate of literacy in the Middle East.

This gradual re-balancing of the activities of the Funds towards more productive projects must also seek mainly to create a greater number of both temporary and permanent jobs. It is well-known that the sector of construction and public works provides substantial leverage to cope with the social disturbances caused by a structural adjustment programme or devaluation. This sector is also crucial in the introduction of a labour-intensive growth policy. To this end, the experiences conducted in the nineties demonstrated that efforts needed to be focused on three priority fields:

- To favour the rehabilitation and maintenance of new constructions;
- To entrust subcontracting to the private sector and reduce reliance on force accounts (works executed by public works departments);
- To favour the use of local resources and labour-intensive technologies (HIMO).

These orientations, the basis of the policy advocated by the ILO in this field for many years, have recently been reaffirmed[32]. They certainly apply in the same way to the range of community works and infrastructures that take their place in Social Funds. Works performed by HIMO methods make a point of engaging temporary, unskilled and under-employed workers, who often find themselves in difficult straits. The modest wage, or standard wage, is fixed as a balance between the supply and demand of local jobs. Consequently, only workers with no other employment possibilities (Subbarao, 1997) are recruited on this type of building site. Social Funds are endowed with significant financial means. Hence, they play an important role in job-creation, since they can gradually increase the percentage of operations involving more productive works. This is even more true as they are designed around the above-cited guidelines.

Naturally, the potential for job-creation is one of the eligibility criteria for Social Fund projects. As previously stated, this factor can probably be taken into better account, especially in Latin America, Central and Eastern Europe and the ex-Soviet Union.

---

32 Creating employment to reduce poverty: the role of employment-intensive approaches in programmes of investments in the ILO's employment-creation programmes, GB.273/ESP/4/1, ILO, Geneva, November 1998.

In the field of job-creation, the same problematic issues plague both the AGETIPs and the Social Funds. These institutions were initially created for this purpose, even if it can be regretted that their temporary status was overemphasised. Nevertheless, until recently, AGETIPs used, in part, an approach geared to the importance of marketable infrastructures that produce revenue for the municipalities. HIMO technologies were encouraged in certain agencies, for example, in road paving projects. It has been observed, however, that certain AGETIPs are generating fewer jobs than was previously the case. They are increasingly forced to compete with other implementing agencies. Deadlines for the completion of works has become a decisive factor and favours the larger and more capital-intensive enterprises.

Yet, Social Funds and AGETIPs are endowed with the main tools needed to foster the development of job-generating projects. It is important for these institutions to regard job-creation as the prime focus for their future development. Indeed, Social Funds are already starting to weight their activities towards more productive projects. On their side, AGETIPs have acquired experience in direct employment-creation. ILO competence can be an added advantage to that existing in both Social Funds and AGETIPs, and promote greater consideration for the employment factor within these institutions.

VI.3 Better training of SMEs and local consulting firms

Social Funds, particularly those in Latin America, neglected the matter of capacity-building for small local enterprises and consulting firms. The most notable exception to this generalization concerns the FID in Madagascar, the PNAS in Rwanda and the Armenian Social Fund. This observation is still valid for AGETIPs world-wide, despite the efforts of certain agencies. Whenever Social Funds and AGETIPs have organised training courses, these were subcontracted to specialized training institutions or to consultants. This training was offered on an ad hoc basis to remedy the flaws that emerged from the studies and work conducted.

There are many reasons why Social Funds and many development bodies call upon SMEs and local consulting firms: some actually prefer to do so or feel they must increasingly do so. These reasons include:

- The pressing need for capacity-building in the local construction industry and to improve the technical knowledge of the managers and site foremen, especially using HIMO techniques;

- The fact that locally-based firms are more likely to recruit on the spot and, thus, facilitate job-creation;

- The use of local equipment goes hand in hand with HIMO techniques and is the source of indirect job-creation;

- Many factors underlie the lowering of costs: a) operation costs and profit margins of SMEs are lower than those of large enterprises; and, b) stiff competition reigns between the SMEs;

- Conducting a variety of small projects scattered around remotely situated areas demands a certain degree of flexibility, which is the strength of local SMEs.

The contribution of these enterprises and of local consulting firms to socio-economic development is considerable when they are well-trained in both technical skills and business management, and when they can properly carry out tenders and contracts that respect specifications and working conditions. The training they are given in these areas must, in theory, meet the following objectives:

- For the SMEs: to fill out the tender documents correctly; to improve the quality of implementation; respect deadlines; ensure proper management of the firm; and, pay workers on time, with due respect for the specifications and for working conditions set out in fundamental ILO Conventions. Frame 13 illustrates a good example of the minimum conditions fixed by the ILO for contractors on projects involving the organization[33];

- For local consulting firms: to conduct good technical studies of the projects so as to facilitate supervision and maintenance of the works; to design projects from an HIMO perspective, using local technologies

---

33 Also refer to D. Tajgman and J. de Veen, 2000, on the work policies and practices in employment-intensive infrastructure programmes.

and equipment; to make accurate cost estimates; and to organise scrupulous technical and financial monitoring of the works;

- For the Client (or Delegated Client): to provide better management of the contracts; and, guarantee proper maintenance and operation of infrastructures and services, once completed.

Frame 13: **Respect of fundamental ILO Conventions on working conditions**
The contract holder is required to:

Regular workers should be recruited in the local area as far as possible. Workers will be at least 18 years of age;
- Women will make up at least 25% of the total workforce on the job;
- Equal pay for equal work will be ensured;
- Equal job opportunity and fair treatment at work will prevail;
- Wage will be paid promptly and integrally to workers and support personnel without any abusive practices;
- Minimum wage set by labour law will be applied;
- Occupational health and safety conditions will be respected on the worksite;
- Necessary precautions will be taken for the prevention of work-related accidents;
- Individual work cards (badges) will be drawn up whenever possible, containing the same date as that provided in the record of wages.

There is a continuous need to assess training requirements on a regular basis, both for Social Funds and AGETIPs in order to improve the performance of various contributors. This helps establish a training plan that is adapted to implementation schedules for the projects. In this respect, it is worth mentioning the training plan recently developed by the ILO in Madagascar[34] for trainers, SMEs, local consulting firms and supervisors. The use of this plan (Bynens, Olivier, 2001) was a condition for the implementation of the Rural Transport Project being launched in Madagascar with the support of the World Bank.

The ILO has just published an HIMO Training Course Intended for SMEs, Local Consulting Firms and State Engineers to meet the needs of Social Funds, AGETIPs or any other large-scale development programmes in this area. This course consists of six training manuals available only in CD format due to the wide range of subjects addressed. These topics include: building and maintenance of rural access roads; paved roads, road system and drainage; construction building; invitations to bid and tendering; enterprise management; and the training of trainers. This training course was designed

[34] This plan is based on a series of seven volumes of methodology and practice of HIMO routes by F. Olivier. It was published by the ILO/NORAD in 1999.

with the help of AFRICATIP, the Association of African Agencies for the Implementation of Works of Public Interest. These manuals deal with invitations to bid and tenders[35], enterprise management and working conditions in the HIMO approach. In these manuals, the issues of payment and occupational safety and health are also addressed.

VI.4 Encouraging the development of micro-financing systems

Social Funds achieved undeniable success in the infrequent cases where they promoted micro-financing operations, such as in the Egyptian Social Fund. These activities generated permanent jobs and were of particularly benefit to women. Moreover, the majority of borrowers were poorer than those who could apply for larger loans from commercial banks. Social Funds could then be increasingly involved in training and helping local credit institutions. They could make up for isolated shortages in this field, given their capacity to intervene in remote and particularly under-equipped regions. It is necessary for Social funds to rebalance their portfolios of projects towards more micro-financing activities, given the results that may be anticipated for sustainable jobs. This type of action is particularly consistent with their mandate.

One of the key activities in micro-financing operations is the development of guarantee funds that enable small and micro-enterprises to obtain bank loans. These guarantee funds reduce the gap between commercial banks, which refuse to take risks, and small contractors. It is clearly advantageous to introduce this type of activity to help local construction and building SMEs. These companies often face great obstacles in their preparations when they cannot obtain credit (D'Hont, van Imschoot, 1997 and Deelen, Osei Bonsu, 2002).

A guarantee fund has better chances of long life if it is decentralized and close to the potential beneficiaries. It is necessary to understand the needs of micro-financing institutions and to provide solid training if the guarantee funds are to preserve sufficient capitalization. This training must focus on the following elements: risk assessment, marketing, minimum capital volume to establish a revolving fund, internal audit and fund management.

---

35 For this aspect, refer also to P. Bendall, A. Beusch and J. de Veen, 2000.

To assist in this task, over the past few years, the ILO has designed a whole range of services for the development of micro-financing systems, which are more specifically geared to the social dimension of these systems. The ILO regularly organizes two-week courses on the Efficient Management of Micro-financing for Small and Micro-enterprises at its International Training Centre in Turin. The ILO further offers a comprehensive training programme which covers Africa and Asia for participants in the new guarantee funds.

VI.5 Responsibility-sharing, decentralization and community-management

It remains a complex process to distribute responsibilities among the various participants involved in carrying out development operations. This is true in most countries which are increasingly engaged in institutional reforms and which have Social Funds. The aim of this process is to distribute authority in a more resourceful manner to obtain a workable decentralization of responsibilities.

Challenges arise from the fact that each category of project has unique requirements. The example of education illustrates this fact well. The proposal to build a school must be approved as part of the national school map or by the Regional Directorate of the Ministry of Education. It is the ministry that is responsible for naming an adequate number of teachers. Then, the role of the decentralized authority is to inspect the quality of education and to allocate subsidies for the purchase of school equipment. This ministry is also in charge of maintenance and operation work in collaboration with the communities and the parents' associations. In contrast, for the rehabilitation of a micro-irrigation scheme, the users' association is the only intermediary. This is the situation of Social Funds that comprise a great variety of projects. Broadly-speaking, these institutions as well as development operations must adapt to situations on a case-by-case basis, while, at the same time, remaining flexible and pragmatic.

The ILO has long been involved in development operations that focus on infrastructure and rural works and employ HIMO methods and local materials to the maximum. From this experience, the ILO gradually developed an effective concept of how best to distribute roles and responsibilities among the different participants. Table 9 presents a

Table 9: The division of roles and responsibilities in small or large-scale works between the various actors		
Participants	**Large-scale works (public works)**	**Small-scale works (community works)**
Individuals	- they are recruited as workers (remunerated jobs) - they benefit from the infrastructure created	- they are recruited as workers (remunerated jobs or volunteer work) - they contribute to the cost of the project and benefit from the infrastructure
Local associations	- they are informed of the project	- they come up with ideas for projects and participate in the preliminary evaluation of proposals - they determine priorities - they introduce Steering or Maintenance Committees - they manage the funds advanced to the Steering Committees - they carry out the projects - they create the users' associations
NGOs	- no role	- they often provide support for local associations during the implementation of the above tasks.
Rural or urban communities	- they prepare the priority investment plans - they contribute to the cost of the project - they benefit from the infrastructure created (market infrastructure) - they are responsible for maintenance	- they sometimes contribute to the cost of the projects and to their maintenance, in addition to the contributions from beneficiaries
Decentralized administrations	- they ensure that the proposals comply with Government policy - additional contributions in human and material resources	- they sometimes start by participating in the training within rural communities, planning priority investments and administering contracts awarded to the private sector, and the maintenance and operation of infrastructures
Small and medium enterprises	- they sometimes work as subcontractors for large enterprises	- they perform projects on behalf of local associations
Large enterprises	- they implement projects for municipalities/communities	- no role
Consultants and large NGOs	- they conduct the technical and socio-economic studies, prepare the tender documents and provide supervision and maintenance	- they often intervene to support associations or to train local NGOs
Management of development projects	- they evaluate and approve requests - they prepare the documents for contract management - they pay the contracting parties - they monitor project indicators - they organize ex-post evaluations	- they evaluate and approve requests - they channel funds in many instalments to local organizations - they supervise and help community projects by offering support structures (NGOs, consultants) - they organize ex-post evaluations

summary of how this distribution should be made, based on its own experience in this sphere. This distribution applies both to small-scale community works and to large-scale works beyond the scope of the community. This experience could be usefully shared with those observed over the years from Social Funds.

The situation is usually more ambiguous for medium-scale works because it is difficult to determine if they are public or community-based. It often occurs that the main channels and works of an irrigation scheme belong to and are maintained by the decentralized administrations of the Ministry of Agriculture, while the secondary and/or tertiary network is privatized with its owners grouped in users' associations. Markets that have been built constitute another example. They belong to the communities, but their management is entrusted to an organization of vendors. Only in cases where local communities and grass-roots organizations have reached a solid agreement can projects operate successfully.

For the above reasons, it is essential to help local communities and the associations develop management skills enabling them to be involved fully in devising and maintaining contracts for small and medium-size works. This approach can rarely be applied to Social Funds developed in Central and Eastern Europe, where there is hardly any network of local associations in existence. It ends up being municipalities which organize the management of small and medium-size projects. This also holds true in Latin America, although they may do so there for other reasons. This process started in Africa about ten years ago with the support of fund providers and NGOs.

Several Funds have tried in recent terms to delegate project implementation increasingly to community organizations, including the award of contracts. An analysis of the projects thus implemented was recently conducted on the Social Funds in Madagascar (FID), Malawi (MASAF), Peru (FONCODES) and Yemen (SFD). This study (Da Silva, 2000) demonstrated the effectiveness of this approach in terms of cost. It also revealed the capacity of these local organizations to mobilize funds equivalent to the subsidies granted by the Fund. Even in cases where the value of the projects managed by the local community rarely exceeds

$50,000, additional training is still needed in the following areas: project management, award of small contracts, accounting and the means of ensuring transparent procedures. The transparency factor can be developed more specifically in the following manner:

- provide information from the community on sums received and expenses incurred;
- post invitations to bid in a public building and make public award of the contracts;
- establish a Supervisory Board within the community.

Among other duties, it is the prerogative of the community to decide whether the project should be conducted by enterprises or by direct labour provided by local petty contractors. In the latter case, the Steering Committee of the project purchases the equipment and hires the vehicles to transport the construction materials. The communities choose to do works by direct labour in almost all cases, in hopes of saving some money. It is essential for the Social Fund to ensure close financial monitoring of the many small contracts made by the local communities, which is a lengthy process. The Fund must launch additional measures, essential in ensuring projects are implemented in a scrupulous and professional manner. These measures, usually for training, are investments in social capital, a key for the future.

For the past ten years, the ILO has been involved in many projects in Africa where the matter of involving direct beneficiaries in the identification, introduction and management of works has become an increasingly pivotal point. The ILO recently published a background document in French on community management of contracts. Entitled Approaches and Practices in Community Contracts: Lessons Drawn from Field Experiences (De Bie, 2002)[36], this document is based on the experiences conducted in the rural and urban areas of seven countries[37].

---

36 This study is based on another document in English which it elaborates on. This document is entitled: Community Contracts in Urban Infrastructure Works (Tournée, Van Esch, 2001)

37 These projects were conducted in South Africa, Madagascar, Mali, Uganda, Senegal, Tanzania and Togo.

It provides a summary of the various contractual approaches used to integrate beneficiary groups into works programmes or projects in urban and rural areas. It could be very useful for the World Bank and the ILO to exchange their experiences in this domain.

CHAPTER 7

Conclusions

VII.1 Overall assessment

Up until the end of 2001, over 100 Social Funds and AGETIPs were operating throughout the world. Some US$ 9 billion had been invested by these institutions. Social Funds arrived in Central and Eastern Europe and in the countries of the ex-Soviet Union (1995), in Latin America (1986), and Africa (early nineties). More recently, they were launched in the Middle East and Asia. Meanwhile, AGETIPs have been confined to Africa. Together, Social Funds and AGETIPs have become powerful instruments to provide countries in crisis or those in economic transition with local social and economic infrastructures and with social services. Their main goal is to improve the living conditions of both rural and urban populations. They are particularly concerned with improving the lot of the most vulnerable. The conclusions below are only a general evaluation of Social Funds and AGETIPs and must be therefore refined in the specific context of each institution.

■ Strong points

o The rapid funding as well as the efficient and scrupulous set-up of a great number of small-size and wide-ranging projects. These projects include small infrastructure works, provision of social services and income-generating activities or micro-financing operations. These all constitute major and pertinent elements in the fight against poverty;

o The involvement from the grass-roots level of populations in identifying and approving projects. Local associations are granted funds for this purpose in order to help them continue their own development process themselves;

o The transparency of their procedures, ranging from the selection of projects to the contract awarding procedures. This ensures these projects greater credibility among beneficiaries and providers of funds;

o Their emphasis on the collaboration of a large number of participants from the administration, civil society and the private sector;

o Their promotion of a national/local construction industry able to create jobs;

o Women are still often the victims of severe discrimination. It is a struggle for them to make themselves heard, and they often derive little benefit from development activities in the majority of the countries where Funds operate. It is natural then to mention those Funds whose projects have benefitted women over the last few years. This should be underlined if one recalls the mixed conclusions of the research programme conducted by the ILO in 1996-1997 to evaluate the specific effects of Social Funds on women. The progress made by the Funds in this area should be saluted, despite the enormity of the tasks ahead;

o The improvement of their means of intervention, enabling them to adapt to changes linked to decentralization and react swiftly to natural disasters, for instance, or in the aftermath of conflicts;

o Their capacity to mobilize additional financial resources, beyond the loans granted by the World Bank and other financial institutions. This capacity is largely due to their low cost of operation when compared with those of similar operations.

■ Weak points

o The limited percentage of projects for job-creation, such as productive infrastructures, micro-credit projects and income-generating activities;

o The minor role given to capacity-building in NGOs and mutual financial institutions, also called intermediaries in Social Fund action, although there has been relative progress recorded in the recent years in this respect;

o The need to improve the process of targeting and identifying key groups despite the progress made. This is a very complex field, however, and, compared with other social development programmes, Social Funds have done relatively well;

o The reduced focus on the creation of temporary or permanent jobs. This is cause for considerable concern as the income thus generated facilitates readier financial handling of the infrastructures. Moreover, figures and data in this respect are insufficient to make an accurate calculation of the impact of projects in this field.

■ **Limitations points**

o The dimension of Social Funds, taken independently of other similar programmes, unfortunately prevents them from having sufficient impact given the severe poverty that afflicts the Social Funds countries. This is true even if they do serve as very valuable models;

o Ensuring the sustainability of the infrastructures and services created supposes that the public and/or decentralized administrations contribute to their subsequent operation and maintenance costs. It is not the task of the Social Funds to make up for the possible deficiencies of these administrations in sector-based projects. The Funds cannot, therefore, fully guarantee a long life for the infrastructures they have supported.

■ **Original points**

o The development model offered by Social Funds is founded on the process of submitting project proposals that adopt a bottom-up approach for project requests. This approach is being increasingly used by development organizations, and is a break away from the traditional pattern of centralized planning. The originality of the Funds on this level stems from the wide application they make of this approach, unlike the above-cited bodies;

o They are endowed with an innovative structure for institutional organization.This has several distinctive features including: a) a large degree of autonomy for management balanced by independent and frequent financial and technical audits; b) the recruitment of highly competent managers, remunerated according to the private sector pay scale; c) management bodies in which the State, civil society and the private sector are represented; and d) detailed Operation Manuals that help personnel to be more effective in their tasks.

VII.2 ILO contribution

This study stressed that the effectiveness of Social Funds and AGETIPs can be improved through more sustained collaboration with the ILO, which enjoys unquestionable comparative advantages in certain areas. This collaboration will facilitate the correction of the above-mentioned weak points, mainly in the following spheres:

■ An integrated rural accessibility planning (IRAP) system

This is a methodology developed in recent years and to which the ILO contributed significantly. This type of approach helps identify the needs, priorities, investments and interventions able to facilitate the supply or availability of social services and basic infrastructures to needy populations. It has been observed that the Funds could draw up a classification of the most urgent needs at the district level in order to set priorities and facilitate better project selection. The ILO has just published a *Guide to Integrated Rural Accessibility Planning in Malawi*, which has an even wider application.

■ A more systematic use of HIMO technologies

The creation of employment is a traditional objective, both within AGETIPs and Social Funds. In practice, many factors limit the results of these institutions in this domain. Within the Funds, the balance is usually tipped in favor of activities that are more productive, employment-intensive and income-generating. However, the implementation of activities that create more jobs, both in the short and long term, implies the works must be subcontracted directly to local associations or to SMEs. It further implies the use of local resources and HIMO technologies. The ILO could certainly contribute much in these areas, given its experience in labour-intensive investment programmes;

■ Training SMEs and local consulting firms

Social funds, especially AGETIPs, strive hard to upgrade the skills of local SMEs and local consulting firms. These efforts could be even more effective if they were organized more systematically and made good use of ILO expertise. The latter has just developed, together with AFRICATIP, an *HIMO Training Course Intended for SMEs, Local Consulting Firms and State Engineers.* This comprehensive course is available on CD. The manuals that deal with invitations to bid, tender submission, and the management of enterprises also include modules on working conditions in the HIMO works, remuneration and occupational health and safety.

■ Structuring the local construction industry

Given the position and leading role Social Funds and AGETIPs have in the local construction industry, these institutions could participate more actively in structuring this sector. This could be done by encouraging the training of small contractors and of local consulting firms using the model advocated by the ILO in Madagascar. These groups could then participate fully in developing training, introducing a system of mutual guarantees and setting uniform rules and standards in the local construction industry.

■ Development of micro-financing systems

Micro-financing operations should assume a larger role in Social Funds, given their impact on sustainable employment and income-generating activities which often benefit women and marginalized groups. They could help develop, among other things, a local network of small construction firms, which is often impeded by their lack of guarantees required to obtain bank credits. The ILO possesses a training know-how in this subject, and has obtained results in operations of this type in Africa and Asia. This training takes the form of regular courses held at the International Training Centre of the ILO in Turin on the *Efficient Management of Micro-financing Institutions of Small and Micro-enterprises.*

■ **Decentralization and community management of the contracts**

The terms and conditions of implementation vary with the size of each project. AGETIPs and Social Funds must ensure that both local communities and decentralized administrations participate in large-scale projects. For the small or medium-scale projects, local associations and small local enterprises are increasingly called upon. When it comes to the community management of projects, the ILO and the World Bank have acquired a certain amount of experience over the past years and been able to develop appropriate tools. In this connection, the ILO has just published a document on this subject entitled: *Community Contracts in Urban Infrastructure Works: Practical Lessons from Experience.* Closer cooperation between these institutions would be welcome in this regard, in order to integrate these contractual approaches firmly within Social Funds and AGETIPs.

VII.3 The future of Social Funds

While Social Funds and AGETIPs are perfectible institutions, they have shown evidence of their originality and effectiveness. Their number is constantly on the rise, and they now operate in the Middle East and Asia. As flexible and rapidly operational instruments, they can benefit poor populations who would otherwise be left by the wayside in development activities. They increasingly call upon local bodies, and thus, contribute significantly to the implementation of Governments' social policy. Under these conditions, they must fulfill three main functions in the years to come, given the circumstances:

■ Sustainable instruments for the reduction of poverty

In the last few years, the World Bank has re-iterated and further elaborated on the general vocation of sustainable social development (Jorgensen, Van Domelen, 1999). These authors insist that Social Funds must give greater weight to projects that can prevent and reduce risks plaguing the most deprived populations, support their capacity-building and enhance their participation. This recommendation is consistent with the conclusions of this study. It implies that a major share of projects be devoted to productive and social projects and to capacity-building of the local communities and their members. It should be considered that the financing of these activities falls under the regular budget of Social Funds. Taking into account the persistent nature of poverty, it is also vital to insist on the essential durability of Social Funds if they are to produce tangible results. Lastly, it is very preferable for Funds to remain independent institutions, mandated by Governments to continue to combat poverty with their characteristic flexibility and efficiency.

■ Debt alleviation

The development of debt alleviation programmes has given rise to the preparation of poverty reduction strategy papers (PRSP) in the past few years. The PRSP programmes are part of the initiative launched in 1998 by the World Bank, the IMF and the main creditor countries to help heavily indebted poor countries (HIPC). The objective is to forgive the debts of a certain number of countries while ensuring they will not fall again into this cycle. The fact is that few institutions seem able to live up to these proposals on a large scale apart from Social Funds, given their restrictions and deadlines. It would be possible in the near future to entrust these effective institutions with management of all or some of these alleviation programmes in addition to their usual activities. One advantage of this new mission is that it would involve Governments further in the direct financing of the Funds.

■ Crisis situation

In case of economic crisis, environmental disasters and in the aftermath of conflicts, it is necessary to set up the most effective programmes as quickly as possible. Granted, this causes the Funds to revert to a circumstantial mission, like that which characterised the first generation of Social Funds. Nevertheless, in the present case, the Funds would benefit from the unmatched experience they accumulated over more than fifteen years. Being lasting instruments for social development, they are at an advantage, given their flexibility and their rapid means of intervention, to respond to emergencies. This would mean, however, special and additional financing to enable them to deal with these kinds of responsibilities.

BIBLIOGRAPHY

Abedian I, 1993, *A Diligent Public Works Scheme Can Deliver the Goods,* Business Day, 19 Feb., South Africa.

Anker R., Bilsborrow R., De Graff D., 1998, *Poverty Monitoring and Rapid Assessment Surveys,* ILO, 96 p.

Bentall P., Beusch A., de Veen J., 1999, *Employment-intensive Infrastructure Programmes : Capacity-building for Contracting in the Construction Sector,* ILO, 228 p.

Berar-Awad A., 1997, *Social Funds Revisited: An Overview with a Particular Focus on Employment and Gender Dimensions,* Action Programme on Economic Reform and Structural Change: Promoting Women's Employment and Participation in Social Funds, 43 p., ILO, Geneva.

Bigio A., 1998, *Social Funds and Reaching the Poor: Experience and Future Directions,* Economic Development Institute of the World Bank, EDI Learning Resource Series, World Bank, Washington D.C.

Bynens E., Olivier F., 1998, *L'approche HIMO et les investissements routiers: Perspectives pour la création d' emploi et l' économie de devises à Madagascar,* ILO, Socio-Economic Technical Papers, No. 3.

Bynens E., Olivier F., 2001, *Rapport de la mission de formulation d'un programme de formation HIMO à Madagascar,* ILO, 77 p.

Chen, Ravallion, 2000, World *Development Indicators 2000,* World Bank.

Contreras M., 1997, *Social Funds: Employment and Gender Dimensions,* ILO, Case Study, No. 1 Spanish, Action Programme, 52 p.

Cornia G., Jolly R., Stewart F., 1987, *Ajustement à visage humain: Protéger les groupes vulnérables et favoriser la croissance,* Paris, Economica, 372 p.

Costa E., Mouly J., 1974, *Employment Policies in Developing Countries,* published on behalf of the ILO by George Allen and Unwin, London, 251 p.

Da Silva S., 2000, *Community-based Contracting: A Review of Stakeholder Experience,* World Bank.

Deelen L., Osei Bonsu. K., 2002, *Equipment Finance for Small Contractors in Public Work Programmes,* ILO Social Finance Programme, Working Paper No. 28.

Del Cid, 1997, Social Funds: *Employment and Gender Dimensions,* ILO, Case Study No. 3, Action Programme, 84 p.

D'Hont Y., van Imschoot M., 1998, *Projet de routes rurales et d'équipement des PME du BTP en appui au développement des régions du Vakinankaratra et de l'Amoron'I Mania,* Madagascar, Rapport principal, ILO, 75 P.

Ebbe K., Narayan D., 1997, *Design of Social Funds: Participation, Demand, Orientation, and Local Organizational Capacity*, World Bank, Discussion Paper No. 375.

ECLAC, 1998, *Social Panoramas of Latin America,* United Nations, Santiago, Chili.

Egger Ph., Garnier Ph. and Gaude J., 1992, *Ajustement structurel et compensation sociale: Etudes de cas au Honduras, Madagascar et Sénégal,* ILO, Occasional Paper No. 11, Interdepartmental Project on Structural Adjustment, Geneva, 30 p.

Garnier Ph., van Imschoot M., 1992, The Administration of Labour-intensive works done by contract: Practical Guide. ILO Geneva, 150 p.

Garnier Ph., Majeres J., 1992, *Lutter contre la pauvreté par la promotion de l'emploi et des droits économiques et sociaux au niveau local,* International Labour Review, ILO, vol. 131, No. 1, p. 69 to 82.

Ghai D. and Vivian J.M., 1992, *Grass-roots Environment Action: People's Participation in Sustainable Development*, London, Routledge.

Goovaerts P., 2001, *Employment and Social Investment Funds in Eastern Europe and Central Asia*, ILO, Socio-economic Technical Papers, 75 p.

Guérin L., 1994, *Cambodia ILO/UNDP Employment Generation Programme. Evaluation Report, Part II.*

ILO, 1987, *High-level Meeting on Employment and Structural Adjustment*, 23-25 November, WEP 2-46-04-03, Geneva.

ILO, 1998, Social Funds: *Employment and Gender Dimensions*, Report on the Technical Brainstorming Workshop, Geneva, Sept. 29 to Oct. 1, 1997.

ILO, 1998, *Job-creation Programmes in the ILO : (a) Employment-generation for Poverty Reduction: The role of Employment-intensive Approaches in Infrastructure Investment Programmes*, GB.273/ESP/4/1, Geneva.

ILO, 2000, *World Labour Report*, Geneva.

ILO, 2000, *A Guide to Integrated Rural Accessibility Planning in Malawi*, ASIST Programme, Geneva.

ILO, 2001, *Cours de Formation HIMO à l'usage des PME, des bureaux d'études et des ingénieurs de l'Etat*, CD Rom (2), Geneva.

Jacobi P., 1991, *Desentralización municipal y participación ciudadana, in Estudios Sociales Centroamericanos (San José)*, no. 55, January-April, pp. 45-60.

Jørgensen S. L., Van Doemelen J., 1999, *Helping the Poor Manage Risk Better: The Role of Social Funds*, World Bank, Conference on social protection and poverty, Inter-American Development Bank, 22 p.

Keir-El Din H., 1997, *Social Funds: Employment Gender Dimensions*, ILO, Case Study No. 2, Action Programme, 50 p.

Lennartson M., Stiedl D., 1995, *Technology Choice: Man or Machine*, Case studies from Lesotho and Zimbabwe, ILO.

Makonnen R., Marc A., Skillings R.F., *The Design of Social Action Programmes under Structural Adjustment*, World Bank Report No. 9344-AFR, 76 p.

Marc A. and al., 1993, *Social Action Programmes and Social Funds: A Review of Design and Implementation in Sub-Saharan Africa*, World Bank Discussion Papers, Africa Technical Department Series, No. 274.

Moncado Vigo G., 1997, Report of the Inter-American Development Bank.

Newsletter, 2000, Social Fund for Development, Yemen, No. 11, July.

Olivier F., 1999, *Cahier des charges-type*, Série méthodologie et pratique de HIMO Routes, Volume III, ILO, Madagascar.

Owen D., Van Doemelen J., 1998, *Getting an Earfull: A review of Beneficiary Assesments of Social Funds*, SP Discussion Paper, No. 9816, 38 p.

Parker A., Serrano R., 1999, *Social Funds, Decentralization and Local Governance*, World Bank, PRMUP, 68 p.

Perez de Castillo, 1998, *Economic Analysis of Social Investment Projects*, World Bank, LCSHD, 20 p.

UNDP, 2000, *Report on Human Development*.

Rawlings L., Sherburne-Benz L., Van Doemelen J., 2000, *Evaluating Social Fund Performance Across Countries: Preliminary Conclusions Based on Oral Presentation*, Conference on Social Funds, World Bank, Washington, 5-7 June 2000.

Razafindrakoto, M., 1999, MAD/HIMO: *Un modèle de simulation de l'impact macro-économique de l'approche HIMO à Madagascar*, ILO, Geneva.

Siri G., 1998, *Participación ciudadana y fortalecimiento de la sociedad Civil: Aportes para un marco de referencia*, Inter-American Development Bank, Washington D.C.

Siri G., 2000, *Employment and Social Investment Funds in Latin America*, ILO, Socio-economic Technical Papers, No. 7, 27 p.

Siri G., 2001, *Targeting Assistance Towards Those Most Affected by Disasters: The Role of Social Investment Funds*, Conference on Innovations in Managing Catastrophic Risks: How can they help the poor ?, World Bank, 29 p.

Stewart F. and van der Geest W., 1994, *Adjustment and Social Funds: Political Panacea or Effective Poverty Reduction ?*, ILO, Employment Papers No. 2, 39 p.

Subbarao K., 1997, *Public Works as an Anti-Poverty Programme: An overview of Cross-Country Experience*, American Journal of Agricultural Economics.

Tajgman D., de Veen J., 1998, *Employment-intensive Infrastructure Programmes : Labour Policies and Practices*, ILO, 240p.

Tendler J., Serrano R., 1999, *The Rise of Social Funds: What Are They a Model of?*

Tournée, J., Van Esch, W., 2001, *Community Contracts in Urban Infrastructure Works :* Practical lessons from Experience, Geneva, 113 p.

Thorndahl K., 2001, *Employment-intensive Reconstruction Works in Countries Emerging from Armed Conflicts:* Guidelines, ILO, Geneva, 116 p.

UPADE; 1989, *Modelo para medir el impacto macro-económico de los proyectos del Fondo Social de emergencia*, Unidad de Análisis de Política Económia, La Paz, Bolivia, mimeo.

Van Imschoot M., 2000, *Study on Employment and Social Investment Funds: Experience in Francophone Africa*, ILO, internal report, 40 p.

Watt P., 2000, *Social Investment and Economic Growth: A strategy to Eradicate Poverty*, An Oxfam Publication, 160 p.

World Bank, 1996, *Republic of Yemen, Poverty Assessment*, Middle East Human Resources Division, Middle East and North Africa Region.

World Bank, 1997, *Portfolio Improvement Programme: Review of the Social Funds Portfolio*, Working Group for the Social Funds Portfolio, 56 p.

World Bank, 1997 (April), *Audit Report on AGETIPs*, report FY 98-54.

World Bank, 1999, *Rapport de fin d'exécution SECALINE*, Madagascar, Crédit 2474. MAG.

Wurgraft J., 1995, *Social Investment Funds and Programmes in Latin America: Their Effects on Employment and Income*, in Employment for Poverty Reduction and Food Security, Edited by Joachim von Braun, IFPRI, Washington D. C.

Yemen, 1999, *Annual Report 1999*, Social Fund for Development.

www.ingramcontent.com/pod-product-compliance
Lightning Source LLC
Chambersburg PA
CBHW072159270326
41930CB00011B/2489